Vicious Circles

a story about survival
in a Czech detention camp

Vicious Circles

a story about survival in a Czech detention camp

by
Elga Marianne Fuchs Huke

DANCINGMOONPRESS
NEWPORT.OREGON

Vicious Circles
© 2005 by Elga Marianne Fuchs Huke

Manufactured in the United States of America
Printed by Newport, Oregon LazerQuick

Published by DANCING MOON PRESS
P.O. Box 832, Newport, OR 97365
541-272-1484
Email: carla@dancingmoonpress.com
www.dancingmoonpress.com

Book Design: Carla Perry
Cover design: Karen Downs
Photo of Elga Huke on page 179: John Curtis Crawford

ISBN: 1-892076-16-0
ISBN 13: 978-1-892076-16-8
Library of Congress Control Number: 2005925218

Huke, Elga Marianne Fuchs
"Vicious Circles"
1. Title; 2. Memoir; 3. World War II aftermath;
4. Czech detention camp

SECOND EDITION

CONTENTS

DEDICATION

I wrote this book in memory of my dear mother,
Hedwig and my sister, Renee, who lived with me
through our year of agony. From their endurance
and faith I drew the strength and hope to survive a
seemingly hopeless situation.

I also wrote this book in memory of my father, Victor
Fuchs, who we lost that year and who will always
live in my heart as the teacher and guide, as the
example and idol he was to me.

Elga Marianne Fuchs Huke
2005

INTRODUCTION

In this story, I touch on relatively unknown historic facts. I am recalling events that occurred in Czechoslovakia after Germany was defeated and World War II officially ended on May 5, 1945 with the signing of a peace treaty on the island of Malta.

At that point, the people of Czechoslovakia saw an opportunity to put an end to the Germanism in their country. To prevent once and for all the possibility that it could be taken over by a German ruler again. Like aftershocks from a devastating earthquake, an uprising against anybody of German descent became a justified tool. Arrests of German citizens, by the thousands, took place. Some people were detained while trying to obtain ration cards, others were taken away by marauding hoards of self-appointed militia. Many were tortured and killed on the spot. Like a fury, anger and destruction raged through the streets of Prague.

Long columns of people, mostly women, children and older men, were herded through the streets, much like Jews had been a few years earlier. This time it was Germans who wore white ribbons on their arms instead of the Star of David. Frightened people with very little luggage pushed baby carriages or carried small children. They were to be taken to unknown destinations. Roughly three and a half million Germans were removed from Czechoslovakia in the following year.

In some cases, the rioting crowds carried their actions to extreme cruelties. They beat and tortured defenseless people, stoned them to death or hung them upside down on trees and set fire to them. Shooting occurred all over the city.

My family, together with our fellow tenants, found refuge in the cellar. A small radio kept us informed of the events on the outside. The Prague radio station had been taken over by Czech militia and according to their reports, German tank troops, still stationed in Southern Bohemia, had not responded to the ceasefire, but moved toward Prague. We listened to descriptions of street fights, barricades being built, and German tanks invading the city.

Calls for help went out over the air, first in French, then in English, appealing to the allies to fight the German tank invasion. But according to the peace treaty, American or British troops were not to come any further than the town of Pilsen in the

Western part of Bohemia. (This decision later influenced the political development of the country considerably. It eventually became one of Russia's satellite states.)

On the third day, the call for help came in Russian: *Govorit Prag – Govorit Praga.* "This is Prague calling."

The Russian Army responded, and on May 8th, truckload after truckload of Russian soldiers, tanks and marching troops poured into the city, just as German troops had done only six years before when Adolf Hitler declared Bohemia and Moravia "German Protectorate" in 1939.

Overpowered by the Russian army, the German tanks withdrew and the uprising quieted down, but the arrests of German citizens went on.

CHAPTER ONE

THE ARREST.

The intense ringing of the doorbell, together with a forceful knock at the apartment door interrupted our noon meal. We looked at each other with alarm.

"Oh, my dear God!" my mother exclaimed.

My sister's big brown eyes filled with tears, and Dad's face turned gray. His eyes were hard and angry. My heart beat way up in my throat and the dog jumped from his basket. With the hair standing straight up on his back, the dog ran to announce, or greet, whoever demanded entrance. The pounding became so vigorous that it sounded as if the door would break down.

"Maybe you better go," mother whispered with fright.

ELGA HUKE

Dad decided to answer.

As soon as he opened the door, six Czech militiamen and two Russian soldiers burst into the hallway.

All of them were heavily armed and they pointed their rifles at us as soon as they entered. Their appearance was as intimidating as their action. Four of the men wore riding britches; horsewhips were stuck in their boots. The rest of their uniforms consisted of military jackets of different origins, even some German outfits, and visor caps with red stars. Two wore baggy pants and big sloppy hats instead of the visor caps. Their grim faces matched their violent intrusion. One of them pushed my father against the wall, and pressed a gun to his throat.

"Where did you shoot from?" he shouted. "Where are your weapons?"

The caretaker of the building stood outside the door, looking sheepish and embarrassed. We had lived in that apartment for more than seven years. He knew us well, and was aware that we had nothing to do with the Nazi Party. He knew that we – of all people – had reason to welcome a change in government. Nevertheless, he had to lead the search party to our apartment since sniper shooting from our area prompted the search of all German suspects.

And search they did.

Fanning out over all the rooms, they turned the place into a disaster area: the mattresses on the beds were turned upside down, the cushions were ripped from the couch and turned over, every closet was emptied and the clothes scattered on the floor, every dresser drawer was pulled out and the contents dumped. "Where are your weapons?" they kept yelling. "Where did you hide your guns?"

Then we heard one of them cry out when he reached my father's study. The others rushed to join him. So far they hadn't found anything that resembled a gun. But in one corner of Dad's room was a collection of daggers and swords he had treasured from his university years as a fraternity brother when fencing had been in great fashion.

"Here it is!" the man yelled. "Here is the evidence!"

Triumphantly, he held up an old Colt .45 which was part of the collection.

"Nobody can shoot with this gun, the pin is broken," my father tried to explain. "Anyway, I didn't shoot at all! Can you see any ammunition?"

Oh, the gun was big and impressive, and I remembered playing cops and robber with it when I was a little girl, barely able to lift it with both of my hands.

The men handed it from one to the other.

"It's sure big enough," said one.

"I've never seen one like it before," stated another.

"Well, if you can't shoot with it, you can always clobber somebody over the head with it!"

Loud laughter followed that remark, but I didn't think it was funny at all.

"In any case," the leader finally concluded, "we better take them into protective custody."

"You mean you are arresting us because you found an old gun that doesn't work?" Dad found the man's reasoning absurd.

"That's part of it – a gun is a gun," was the answer. "But since you are Germans, you never know what the mob out there might do to you. So we are going to protect your lives. You may each pack a suitcase. You probably won't come back for a while."

There was a strange undertone in his voice, and he had a nasty grin on his face.

All during the search, I was standing in the living room, petrified. I had grabbed the collar on my dog's neck when Dad went to the door. The hair on the dog's back was still standing straight up. He showed his teeth and his growling became more and more threatening. He was ready to defend what was ours at the slightest command. However, we had no choice but to go, and the caretaker, who was familiar with the dog, took him out of my hand and led him to the door.

"I will take care of him till you come back," he promised. I felt these were empty words and tears ran down my cheeks when my pet turned around in the doorway to give me a last goodbye look.

The past two weeks had been days of fearful anticipation and the danger of being arrested had become very real. The caretaker and our fellow tenants had been quite indifferent. They knew our background but since we spoke German, they didn't know what to do, and certainly none of them could be trusted. Nevertheless, they had vouched for us, and after several searches of our apartment, we had been allowed to stay there for the time being.

Since the turmoil had almost ceased after the Russians occupied the city, we had gone back to our apartment. The market and stores had reopened and it seemed safe enough for me to venture outside to do some shopping. I spoke Czech fluently, so the chance of being recognized as German was slim.

The market was only two blocks away and as I crossed the first street, I noticed a large crowd on the sidewalk. Cheering and shouting, they drove arrested Germans on – to take down a barricade. An overturned streetcar was uplifted with ropes and bare hands. With bleeding fingers, women and children clumsily put cobblestone after cobblestone back into the pavement. Three or four men stood over them, with horsewhips. I was so frightened that tears came to my eyes. My heart went out to the crying children.

I had hurried on. The market was busy. It looked almost normal and I hastily did my shopping. On my way back to the apartment I tried to avoid the street I had passed before, and walked a different route. But again I encountered a large assembly of people. They surrounded a person, shouting and arm-waving as they demonstrated a scornful enthusiasm. All of a sudden, the whole group dispersed.

My feet were glued to the ground and terror ran through my body.

A flaming living torch!

They had poured gasoline over a woman and

put a match to her. With animal-like screams, she rolled on the ground, trying to extinguish the flames that already had penetrated her clothing. The people around her cheered, as if they were watching a boxing match.

How was this possible? How could humans do such a thing? I was so terrified, I couldn't move.

"This is not a sight for a young lady to see." A voice next to me tore me away from this horrible event.

"You better go home," the man continued.

I wondered what he would say if he knew I was German, too. My eyes wide open in dismay, I felt the blood withdrawing from my face, and on shaky knees, I ran home as fast as I could.

But the unrest in the streets was far from over. For several days we heard sporadic shooting from rooftops by desperate German elements, and one of these incidents, happening in our neighborhood, was what led to the arrest of my family on May 23rd.

After the man told us to pack, I went nervous and trembling into Mother's room.

"What shall I put in my suitcase?"

"Just pretend you are going on a trip," Mother suggested. She picked some clothes off the floor where the men had thrown them when they pulled her dresser drawer out.

"Make sure you take some warm underwear, and don't forget your toothbrush! Renee, help the little one," she instructed my sister. "I will see what I can do for Dad."

As always, she was in control of things, even in this upsetting situation. To call me "the little one" was a carryover from younger years. And since my sister was five years older than I, the description seemed appropriate, despite the fact that I was eighteen.

We were given fifteen minutes to do our packing and not everything I threw in my suitcase made sense: an extra dress, slacks, toothbrush, soap, and boots.

The apartment looked a shambles with the unfinished dinner left on the dining room table. But it didn't seem to matter and we were never to come back again to clean it up.

CHAPTER TWO

TERROR.

The six militiamen escorted us to a nearby school that served as a temporary collecting site while it was decided where the families were to be transported. The desks and chairs had been taken out of the classrooms and were piled on top of each other in the hallways.

Upon our arrival, we were each handed a white cloth band to put on our left arm. Then we were separated from our father and our suitcases were searched. Anything that seemed of value to the searching person went into his pocket.

I had packed a pair of felt boots, one of the less sensible things to take in the month of May.

They were practically new and I loved them dearly, for Dad had given them to me on my last birthday.

"Uh," exclaimed the man in delight. "*Huculky!*" Boots!

"They belong to my daughter," my mother protested.

"Oh, no," was the answer. "They are mine now!"

But Mother wasn't going to give up so easily and she reached for the boots. The pleased look on the man's face made room for his angry grimace.

"I tell you what you need," he yelled. And with that his whip came down on my mother's back.

That was too much for me.

Before I could think, I jumped up and my fingernails penetrated the skin on his face. I felt no fear at this point and I was wild with anger.

There was dead silence in the room.

I had broken the skin on both of his cheeks slightly, and when he wiped over them with his hands, drops of blood were on his fingers. For a moment he was surprised. Obviously, he was not used to resistance from young, frightened girls. His face turned red, and a blue vein formed on his forehead.

"*Kočka!*" he yelled. You cat! And a burning pain came over my face. Now he had used the whip on me. I fell to the floor and everything became black around me for a moment.

But very fast I was back on my feet. Back for more. But this time he was ready for me. I didn't realize how senseless my rage was until he hit me again, harder this time, hard enough to keep me on the floor. His whip came down on me again, and again, and again. Mother tried to stop him by catching his arm, only to be struck down herself. The other women and Renee watched in dismay. They didn't know what to do. And when my sister cried out "Please, don't hit them anymore!" he raised his whip at her, too.

He finally quit when Mother and I lay half unconscious on the floor. Then, he walked triumphantly out of the room with my boots as a trophy for his "victory" under his arm.

The welt on my face began to swell and a wet handkerchief brought little relief. Mother's back was red and swollen and we tried to cool her skin too.

We stayed at the school that night, sitting on the floor or lying down, using our suitcases for pillows, trying to get some sleep. Our coats doubled for blankets, for even though it was May, the nights were still quite cool and there was no heat in the building.

The next morning, my sister and I were chosen, with a number of other young women, to line up in the hallway. It was impossible to imagine what was going to happen next.

There were only a dozen of us, and when we moved out onto the street, four armed men accompanied us. Crowds started to gather as soon as we left the building and the guards had their hands full to keep the mob from physically attacking us. What they couldn't prevent was the spitting and shouting. The guards marched us through a number of streets.

At the head of the column was a man with his hands tied behind his back. Most of the crowd's attention was directed at him. He wore a sign on his back and one on his chest. "Traitor" it read on one sign, and "Collaborator" on the other. His clothes were in rags, obviously torn violently. His head was completely shorn. His walk was unsteady and frequently one or the other guard helped him along with a poke of his gun.

"I am scared, Renee," I whispered to my sister.

"I am, too!" She squeezed my hand. "Hold on tightly!"

Her grip gave me a sense of security and it lessened some of my fear knowing that she felt the same as I.

I thought this march would never end but we finally stopped at a low building. Letting us women stand and wait, the guards took the man inside. I couldn't tell if he was beaten or tortured, but by the sound of his screams, there was probably not much difference. When he was brought out after a while, he was staggering, and two of the men had to hold onto him. His face was covered with blood and as he came closer to our group, I saw that one of his eyes was badly inured. In fact, the blood originated there.

I almost became sick to my stomach, and most of the women around me cried out in terror and fear. Strangely enough, none of the men harmed us or even talked to us. We just had to walk through the streets with this poor man. As the signs on his chest and back indicated, he had been working in some way with the Germans and this was his punishment.

The walk back to the school was as long and unpleasant as the way to the low building, and we were glad when we finally returned to the room where our mother was eagerly waiting for us. She was very upset about something and we could tell she had been crying.

"What happened, Mutti?"

She started to cry again and then she told us. The man who had beaten us the day before came back, took her to a latrine and made her clean it. But it wasn't just the simple brushing of a toilet.

There were three stools and every one of them was badly soiled with human excrement all over the rims.

"He didn't give a brush or pail," she sobbed, "but told me to clean it with my hands!"

The thought of this repulsive harassment brought shivers to my back and shakily I tried to dry her tears. She paused for a while to catch her breath.

"I used my handkerchief to remove the mess, and then I had to throw up. Just smell my hands!" she cried out.

And then she added in despair, "and now I don't have a handkerchief!"

CHAPTER THREE

THE INTERROGATION.

That same afternoon, our names were called and we were joined by our father.

"My God, what happened to your face?" he cried out when he saw me.

Mother took his arm.

"You don't want to know," she said. Good thing the dress covered the marks on her back. Dad never found out about that.

We didn't have to walk this time, but were loaded into a police car to be taken to downtown police headquarters.

"Wait here," a man commanded as he led us into a large room. Another man stood at the door, pointing his rifle at us.

"Tell me, what...." Dad started, but the man interrupted him.

"No talking!" he yelled.

"We sat there, an uncomfortable quiet surrounding us, looking at each other in consternation, anxiously awaiting what might happen next.

A half-hour had passed when an officer came to take our father out. He left his suitcase with us, thinking that he would come back soon, as did my mother and Renee, who were called out one by one an hour later.

To overcome my fear of being there all by myself with this fierce-looking man and his gun, I tried to think of something pleasant. I remembered the time when we lived in Vienna, Austria.

We had to leave Germany in 1933 and Dad rented a small house in Nussdorf, a suburb of that beautiful city. Grandfather had owned the Imperial Royal Court Pharmacy there, and it was like coming home for Dad after many years away. He had grown up in Vienna, had studied at the university there, and still had many good friends.

To my great delight, Grandmother, who still lived in Vienna, was going to share the house with us. It was a two-story home, not just an apartment. A white picket fence surrounded a lovely yard. In a wild rock garden by the road, I could watch lizards and salamanders bathing in the sun.

Under the kitchen window, Mother turned an area into a small vegetable garden and there was a little garden house in one corner. That structure became my playhouse and I spent many hours there with my dolls and friends. It was just like paradise for me after always living in an apartment, sharing a room with my sister. Here, I shared the upstairs with Grandma, but had a room for myself. It was a small room and had a slanted ceiling, but it was cozy, and it was mine.

There was a nice view over the front yard and in the winter, swarms of chickadees gathered on my windowsill where I put birdseeds and breadcrumbs. Renee had her own room too, of course. It was on the main floor and she even had her own desk.

Grandmother was a real sweetheart. I hadn't known her very well until then, and we had a wonderful time while we lived together. The fabulous "once-upon-a-time" stories she could tell, her dancing blue eyes, and the mane of white hair that framed her wrinkled face will always be in my memory.

And then there was Daddy's Cherry Tree. It had the most wonderful cherries and Dad strung his hammock under it for his afternoon naps. We would tease him for having it put there so he could have the delicious fruit fall right into his mouth.

I attended a little school a short bus ride away, in Kahlenbergerdorf on the bank of the Danube River. About one hundred steps led to the top of the hill into the building.

The view from there across the river was breathtaking, and the inspiration for many day dreams. However, to my surprise, I found out that the Danube wasn't blue at all! At this point, in Vienna, it was brown and muddy.

A growling noise from my stomach interrupted my pleasant thoughts. The man by the door started grinning – from ear to ear.

"You will talk better when you are hungry," he said.

The waiting, the hunger, and above all the uncertainty about what might have happened to my family made me very nervous and I was close to tears when I was finally called.

"How come you have four suitcases?" I was asked.

"They are not all mine. Three of them belong to my parents and my sister," I explained.

Then I burst into tears. "Where are they? Where did you take my family?"

"Don't ask stupid questions!" A hard poke with is gun emphasized the man's answer. I cried out, but he only laughed and pushed me down the hallway. He had picked up two of the suitcases and told me to take the other two.

"They have to be registered," he explained, "because you are going to an orderly jail."

This time I didn't ask the questions aloud.

Why jail? And what is an "orderly" jail?

We stopped at an office where a policeman put labels with my name on the luggage. Then they led me into another room. An older man sat at a desk, bent over some papers. He was in civilian clothes and apparently had no gun or any other weapon. Sitting there, he appeared to be a rather small man and his hair was very thin, leaving a large portion on the back of his head completely bare. He looked at me over a pair of rimless glasses that sat halfway down on his nose and pointed without a word for me to sit down on a small bench in front of his desk. Then he went back to reading.

Probably only minutes passed, but it seemed longer than the hours I had just spent in the other room.

Finally he spoke: "Name."

"Elga Fuchs."

He looked up. "That is a Jewish name. I thought you were German."

"I am."

He chuckled. "A German Jew!"

"I am not a Jew!"

He gave me a long look, to study my face, then he changed the subject.

"What is your father's occupation?" he asked.

"He is an actor."

"Theater?"

"Yes, and radio."

"An actor in the radio – how about that? How did he do that?"

"He spoke in a microphone and also directed radio plays." I was proud of my Dad and this man obviously never listened to a radio play.

"The German radio station of Prague?"

"Yes."

"How come he wasn't in a concentration camp, since he is Jewish?"

"He isn't Jewish, only half. His father was

Jewish. I guess he never spoke about it. And then he was on the front with troop entertainment, so they couldn't reach him."

"They?"

"The Gestapo."

Again, a long inquisitive look over the rim of his glasses.

"Was he a member of the Nazi Party?"

"No."

"Why not?"

"I don't know, he just wasn't. Not every German was a Party member. He considered Hitler a megalomaniac."

"Were you in the Hitler *Jugend*?"

I hesitated.

"Well, were you?"

"Yes, we all were."

"Who is we?"

"All the kids in school. We had to."

"When your father wasn't a Party member, how come he let you join this outfit?" He raised his voice this time.

"Actually, he was very upset about it, but he had no say in the matter. We were all swept away."

"Did you like it?"

"What?"

"Did you like being one of Adolf Hitler's children?"

I thought for a moment. What was this man up to?

"Well, did you like it?""

"We had a lot of fun."

"Tell me about that, what kind of fun?"

"We learned a lot of songs and had great sports events. I was on the track team and we went to weekend camps where we had wonderful times, running in the woods. I also was a member of the handball crew," I added.

"Didn't your leaders object to you, since you are Jewish?"

"I am not Jewish!"

"All right, part Jewish then."

"They didn't know; neither did I. We are Lutherans."

"So, when did you find out?"

"Not until I was dismissed from the army."

"The army?" His glasses slipped off his nose. "You were in the German army, too?"

"Yes, my year was drafted in 1943."

"Girls, too?"

"Yes."

"But you were still in school!"

"Yes. We finished what they called a 'War-graduation.'"

"Did you wear a uniform?"

"No. I became a civilian employee and was exempt from combat duty."

"Then what?"

"I was dismissed when they found out that I had a Jewish grandfather."

"But they didn't put you in a concentration camp."

"No."

"How come?"

"I don't know. I guess they didn't get around to it. The war was almost over."

He put his glasses back on his nose.

"Interesting story," he mumbled.

After a while, he said without looking at me, hardly raising his voice: "Take your clothes off."

I was so stunned, I couldn't move. He repeated his order and when I still did not react, he got up. "I see I have to get someone to help you."

He rang a little dinner bell on his desk and two other men walked in. They wore civilian clothes too, but one of them wore riding britches like the men before, and he had a whip stuck in his boot.

Before I knew it, my skirt was pulled down. My panties went right with it. My shirt blouse was unbuttoned by one of them, while the other held onto my hands to prevent any interference on my part. They must have done this kind of undressing before, judging by the speed and skill that they displayed in fulfilling the commissar's order.

I was ready to sink into the floor. Never before had I been in front of a man in the nude, and now there were three of them feasting their eyes on my body and enjoying my embarrassment.

When at last they got my bra off, one of them exclaimed: "Dear Lord, is she skinny!"

Then they held each piece of my underwear against the light, inspecting the seams.

What in the world are they looking for?

As soon as they finished their strange investigation and decided that I was too skinny for further abuse, they told me to put my clothes back on. Sobbing, I gathered my things and got dressed. Two of the buttons on my blouse were lost in the process and, even though it was only a small calamity, under the circumstances it was a big loss for me.

The commissar went back to his desk, and the other two men left the room.

And there I sat again – waiting – wondering what would happen next.

Then a woman stepped into the room. She wore a police uniform with a rather tight skirt that barely covered her knees. Gray stockings matched an ugly pair of gray shoes, and a smart little cap sat on her short hair. The stern look on her face and her cold steel-blue eyes frightened me more than any of the men I had encountered in the past two days.

Rigidly she grabbed my arm and led me out of the room. We went down a flight of stairs, obviously into the basement. She opened a heavy door and we walked through a long corridor. I saw one door after another, just as heavy as the one we had passed. Each of them had a little square window with bars.

Jail cells!

An icy feeling grabbed my chest. Bony fingers seemed to get hold of my throat, making breathing difficult. In my imagination, the gray cement floor turned into moist stones of a dungeon. Rats and cockroaches ran over the wet floor and the steel doors appeared to be made of heavy oak, set deeply into the walls.

For a brief moment I stopped.

"Come on, you German pig!" She dragged me more than I walked until we finally came to a table where another policewoman had taken up a position. I was turned over to her, and again we started walking through hallways and around corners.

This has to be a bad dream, I thought. I must wake up soon!

We finally stopped at one of the cells. She opened the door and shoved me in. I couldn't see anything at first. The room was barely lit with a single light bulb hanging from the ceiling, but gradually my eyes became accustomed to the darkness. After a while I could distinguish long staggered benches. The room was fairly large and about fifteen women sat, stood, or walked up to get a better look at me.

I stood there by the door, hopelessly lost and too frightened to say anything. My eyes were swollen from tears and the welt on my cheek reminded me painfully of the things that had happened during the past two days.

What happened next almost made me forget our desperate situation. Was it fate? Was it God's will? Had a spark of humanity inspired one of our tormentors to put our names together?

I heard my sister Renee's voice: "Mutti, it's Elgi!"

Out of the dark, Mother and Renee rushed to hug and kiss me. We could hardly believe that something good actually happened on this terrible day.

We were all together again!

VICIOUS CIRCLES

Some hope came back into our lives, knowing that whatever would happen next, at last we were together!

If only our father could be at our side!

CHAPTER FOUR

WHY?

Through the small barred window, a crack of daylight appeared and a new day broke – the third day of our arrest. It became the longest day of absolute nothing and during the long idle hours we tried to find a reasonable explanation for why this was happening to us. Was it a reprisal for the injustice done to the Jews in Nazi Germany? Or was there some other reason? Was it the age-old hate against all that was German that came to the surface after centuries of oppression?

All through the time of the Holy Roman Empire Bohemia was ruled by German kings. Then, it was part of the Austro-Hungarian Monarchy. At the end of the First World War, their yearning for independence was fulfilled. Czechoslovakia became an independent Republic in 1918 with Thomas G. Masaryk as the first president. The German minority consisted of four million people at the time, a number that could not be ignored in a country where the whole population amounted to only fourteen million. In 1920, a "Language Law" was established, declaring Czech the official language of the land. However, the right to use their native tongue in government, courts and schools was given to the communities where the German population exceeded twenty percent.

In time, these rights were badly abused by the Czech government: German gendarmes were replaced by Czech police and German schools were closed. Sudden ignorance of the German language by Czech officials when communicating in courts infuriated the German people.

By 1936, Adolf Hitler had risen to great power in Germany, and the Germans in Czechoslovakia formed a Party much in favor of his ideas. Unrest and dissatisfaction, mainly in the Czech border district of the "Sudetenland," led to Hitler's threat of war. To prevent that, the annexation of the "Sudeten" to the Reich was decided in an agreement between France, England and Germany in Munich during September 1938.

In March of 1939, the circle was closed when Hitler occupied Czechoslovakia and the country was once again under German dictatorship. A German Governor was put at the head of the state and the Czech people got to know a brute force with a severity they had never experienced before. Czech universities were closed, professors and students arrested. German became the official language and German schools were re-opened.

To complete the terror, Adolf Hitler expanded the persecution of the Jews to this part of his domain. All of them were forced to wear yellow Stars of David on their chests. Streetcars and restaurants became off limits to Jews. Their belongings and businesses were taken away and sold to German Party members for very little money. Most were arrested and taken away. Many of our friends vanished in the middle of the night and were never seen again. Some luckier ones made a quick decision, left their homes and fled to England or the "New World."

During World War II, Czech men were recruited and shipped to labor camps in Germany to work in weapon factories.

In 1942, underground resistance led to the assassination of the German Governor Heydrich, and as a reprisal, the village of Lidice was savagely destroyed. The town's entire male population was exterminated.

These and other events stirred the hate and resentment of the Czech people against German rule to a higher and higher degree, and when Germany was defeated, the time seemed right for an uprising.

The century-old hatred surfaced and my family and I were caught in the turbulence and like other German citizens, we were arrested and ended up in this dark cell.

The door was opened only to bring us food. Bread and water in the morning, and a strange-tasting potato soup served in a mug-like container arrived around noon. Coffee and a sandwich in the evening. It seemed like the day would never end.

In order to keep busy, we tried to get acquainted with the other women. None of them had we known before and not all of them were Germans. They were Czechs, like the man in the school the day before who had sympathized with the Germans, and consequently were marked as collaborators.

Chapter Five

Good-Bye, Dear Daddy!

The next day didn't start any differently from the first one, except instead of potato soup, we received barley. I can still feel the dishwater taste in my mouth when I think of it.

After lunch, the door opened again and one of the matrons yelled: "*Fuchsova!*" the Czech version of our name.

We all three responded.

"There are three of you?" she asked. "Well, I want only one. Elga, you come with me."

"But I just got here, where will you take me?" I wasn't about to give up my newly found family, and clung to my mother's arm.

"Don't worry," she responded. "You aren't

going very far and I will bring you back here in due time."

I had many questions on my mind, but didn't dare to ask for fear of being hit again. My ribs still felt the gun from the day before and my face was swollen and red from the mark the whip had left.

Where is she going to take me, and will she really bring me back to my mother and Renee? I could hardly walk and her firm grip on my arm didn't improve the situation one bit.

All of a sudden the thought of our father pressed its way into my mind. I would have given anything to know where he was, and little did I realize that I was about to find out as the matron led me through the hallway.

We came to a large room filled with people and a lot of noise. My eyes were not quite used to the bright light after spending the last two days and nights in a barely-lit cell. What I could make out through a cloud of heavy smoke were three big oak desks. The walls were covered with posters of communistic slogans and hammers and sickles. An oversized picture of Lenin hung next to a smaller one of the Czech President Benes on the far side. Two large windows reaching almost to the dirty hardwood floor let bright sunshine in. But it could hardly penetrate the smoke.

A man who seemed in charge asked me a question, but his voice was drowned out by all the tumult around us.

He was dressed like the men who had arrested us, and clutched a horsewhip in his gloved hand. The cap on his head was of Russian origin with a red star on the visor. First, I thought he was a Russian, but the way he spoke the Czech language made me realize that he was a member of the Czech militia, and he obviously filled an official position. His mouth was topped by a large mustache, and his bushy eyebrows and his angry, sparkling eyes completed a horrifying picture.

"I want to know if this is your father's suitcase," he yelled into my ear.

His big bony hand gripped my arm as he guided me to a pile of luggage. Most of the suitcases were labeled and had nametags. One of them was opened and I recognized it as my father's. The contents had obviously been searched, part of his belongings were scattered on the floor. From a previous operation, Dad had an open wound to tend and dress, and some of the things he packed when the militia group arrested us were dressing material and cotton strips.

However, most of that was gone.

"Will you finally answer, girl?" the man yelled again, emphasizing his question with another very painful grip on my arm.

"*Ano*," I replied in his language, "yes, but most of the cotton is missing."

All of a sudden, all my fear was gone! I was angry, very angry. In a flash I thought of all the things that had happened during the last three weeks. The end of the war on the 5th of the month, the signing of the peace treaty between Russia, England and America, splitting Germany into pieces like a pie. The start of the uprising, the suffering and tears, the torture and deaths, the rubble and debris. All the riots came to my mind, the turmoils and gatherings of mobs, picking individuals as their victims, to beat or stone to death. The living torch I had witnessed flared through my memory!

I came to realize that the events of the last three weeks, and especially the incidents of the last three days, had built a wall around my feelings. A dullness had taken over, which cushioned any emotional and physical attacks on my person. I hardly felt the burn of the riding whip on my back.

When the officer repeated his questions and added, "I didn't ask you what was missing," my temper swelled again. The tears stuck in my throat until they came to my eyes. A desperate bravery, backed by the fact that Dad had to be somewhere near, since his suitcase was here, made me stand up against this brutal man.

"Where is my father?" I yelled back. "What have you done to him?" But before anybody could answer me, I saw him.

A group of ten or twelve men was standing at attention on the other side of the room. Their faces looked drawn and were covered with heavy beards. Their eyes were dull and expressionless and, resulting from maltreatments and beatings, many of them had crudely-wrapped bloodstained bandages around their heads and arms. A number of them had their clothes partially ripped off their bodies, and all the men looked dirty and neglected.

Dad stood in the front row.

In spite of all the people, our eyes met across the room, and before the whip could strike me again, I tore away from my tormentors, trying to break through he crowd.

My voice was gone. I couldn't even utter what was in my heart. I just wanted to find his wide, protective chest that so many times before had given comfort and shelter against all kinds of problems and troubles. I wanted to feel his strong hands that knew so gently how to stroke, hands that had dried rivers of tears all through my childhood.

At the same time, I felt it was my turn to give him comfort, to hold his hand and to encourage him not to lose faith and to keep up his good spirit.

"Nothing is so bad that it couldn't be worse," he used to say. And, "Tomorrow, all will be well!"

I wanted to believe that, but in this situation, it didn't apply. As it turned out, from now on, many tomorrows were much worse before they got better.

Two of the militiamen grabbed my arms before I could reach the other side of the room, to even touch Dad's fingertips.

The reaction from my father wasn't quite as emotional. He had his feelings better under control than I. He didn't move his feet, but his broad shoulders straightened. He lifted his head and stretched his arms toward me. His eyes were not dull and expressionless anymore, but sparkled with millions of diamond tears that rushed over his unshaven face. Only a moan that had all the love and feelings in it, feelings that we had always felt for each other, came from his pale lips.

My eyes didn't burn anymore for the tears had finally cooled them while they were running over my cheeks.

"Oh *Vati*," was all I could whisper, but I don't think he could hear me. "Oh, my dear Daddy!"

I made one more attempt to get closer, but the iron fists of the two men changed my mind. I cried out from the pain, but offered no more resistance. I didn't want him to see them strike me again. It took little effort to lead me out of the office into the gray hallway where the matron took hold of my arm to take me back to the cell.

We walked back the same way we had come, through hallways, around corners, past countless cell doors. I was in a trance and I didn't feel the gloominess of the surrounding as I had felt it before. The woman next to me was just another person and all I could think was to wake up from a bad dream.

My whole life had taken a rude turnabout. My plans and dreams seemed shattered, and this last farewell from my father made everything collapse completely. For deep down in my heart I felt I would never see him again.

CHAPTER SIX

PRISON.

There wasn't much I could tell my mother and Renee when I arrived back in the cell.

"I saw Dad! Oh Mutti, he looked so hopeless and desperate. He cried, and I could not help him!"

Then the events of the past hour caught up with me and I broke down. My sister held my hands, and Mother took me in her arms.

"Shh, shh," she stroked my head and rocked me as she had done many times when I was small.

"We'll make it through this, I promise we will. As long as we have each other." Crying herself, she kissed my tears away and, clinging together with Renee, we found solace in each other's presence.

As it turned out, we didn't have much time to linger in our pain. The cell door opened and a tall man, dressed and armed like the rest of them, stepped in.

"You are all transferred to better quarters," he shouted. "Get your things together and claim your suitcases on the way out." Somehow, I didn't like the tone of his voice.

Outside the building, fifty other women were already assembled. As soon as we joined them, the whole troop started moving down the street. Silently, my mother clutched my hand while she carried her suitcase in the other one. Renee and I joined hands over my luggage. We wanted to make sure that we would not be separated again.

It was about three o'clock in the afternoon. The streets were fairly busy and people lined up on the sidewalks to watch our trek. Frequently, one or the other person stepped into our path spitting and shouting:

"Kill the German pigs!"

"Drown them in the Moldau River!"

Some tried to snatch the luggage from our hands. It was like running the gauntlet. However, since we were guarded by a large number of armed men, we were relatively safe against bodily assaults.

The march took us about five blocks through the busy center of Prague, delaying traffic and causing hordes of spectators to follow our trail. We ended up at a large building on *Carlovo Namesty*, the Charles Square. It was a prison for women.

We walked up the steps into the building and

after we were registered and had turned our suitcases in, we were led to a small cell. The cots and whatever other furniture might have been in there had been removed. The only equipment I could see was a small stand with a washbasin and a pitcher with water. In the corner by the door was a toilet stool. No chair, nor bench or table. The ceiling was very high and a small window at the top of the room let a bit of light through the bars. Now I knew what the undertone in the guard's voice meant when he told us that we were being taken to "better" quarters.

"*Jedna – dwa – tri – ztiri*," counted the matron, one, two, three, four, pushing one of us into the cell with each count. She stopped at ten, then the heavy door closed with a depressingly dull thud. At the same time, all outside noise seemed to be cut off. Only the breathing of ten frightened women was in the air. Then one started sobbing:

"What's going to happen to us?"

"Let's sit down first," my mother suggested.

We sat on the floor, and it became very crowded. There were ten of us in a cell that was big enough for only two.

"They will probably take us out of here pretty soon. This is too small for ten women for any length of time."

"But how long will we be here?"

"What will they do to us?"

These and a hundred other questions were asked, but nobody knew the answers.

We tried to settle down and get acquainted. Two of the women were originally from Germany, evacuated with their families from bombed cities to safer territory within Czechoslovakia. During the turmoil of the uprising, both of them were separated from their children and taken into custody the same way as my family and I were. Neither of them knew where her children were.

While we were still trying to understand what was happening, the door opened again but instead of taking somebody out, two more women were pushed into the room.

"My goodness, we are so crowded already! You can't put any more in here!" one of us exclaimed. The matron did not take very kindly to that remark.

"Oh, yeah?" she laughed. "You don't think so, huh? You better shut up or I'll show you what I can do!" With that, she swung her billy club in a very unfriendly manner. We were stunned.

She wouldn't really use the thing, would she?

None of us said it, but I am sure it went through everybody's mind. The two new women were standing by the door, just as frightened as the rest of us. The door closed again.

It was the end of May, and the days were getting warmer. The little window was closed and the air became rather stuffy. The day grew darker outside, but nobody knew what time it was. Our watches and jewelry were taken away together with our suitcases when we entered the building.

After a while a light bulb on the ceiling was turned on and it gave a dim light. The door was opened again and two matrons appeared in the doorway. With them were two girls in shapeless gray gowns.

"Chow time," one of them announced cheerfully, and handed each of us a metal cup. The other one filled it with a black liquid out of a big kettle, just like in the other jail. They said it was coffee. It even looked somewhat like coffee, but the first gulp made us realize that plain water would have been a better choice. It tasted awful!

As the younger one of the matrons handed us each a small loaf of bread, her eyes seemed to apologize and she said in a gentle voice:

"Don't eat it all at once. You won't get another one until tomorrow night."

It was her eyes that caught my attention for they were the bluest blue I had ever seen, with a sad and questioning look. It was as if she were as puzzled about our presence here as we were, and could not understand why we were in captivity. I was wondering why she would be a matron in a prison; her pleasant manner was in contrast to the job she was doing. It became clear to me that she felt strongly about the way we were treated, but was fearful of letting her feelings be known.

Nobody spoke – it was just too incredible to say anything. The sound of the closing door was to become a trying experience for the next four weeks. The whole thing was a nightmare. I was sure I would wake up soon and all would be well.

But it was all too real!

Who would have thought three weeks ago that it would end this way? Or was it the end?

The next morning, the door was opened only to serve us another ladle-full of the black liquid, and around noon, our containers were filled with some kind of soup that had a few potatoes floating in it. We could hardly wait for the evening when we were going to get another piece of bread. By that time we were all so hungry, all we could think of was food.

"I am going to have ten scrambled eggs when we get out of here," Julia, a young woman in her twenties, planned.

"I could go for one or two pork chops," my sister chimed in. For me, beef roast and dumplings seemed a fair choice. And so we were all dreaming of something good and nourishing to eat.

After the second day, most of us became sick. Vomiting with an empty stomach became a painful, daily routine.

To make the small piece of bread last longer, we tried different ways of stretching it. To eat just a little bite at a time in order to have something all day took an enormous amount of willpower. But we needed all the power we had to keep us from losing our minds. So everybody just devoured the little nourishment with one gulp. We felt some satisfaction for a short while, only to be even more hungry after that.

The best way to make the precious morsel last was just to keep chewing it. That way we could have something in our mouths for hours and somehow even our stomachs were fooled that way. We made a game of it, to see who could chew the longest on a bite without swallowing it.

The small cell was our living quarters for the next four weeks. The crowded condition with twelve women in that tiny room presented an enormous problem. At night, only ten of us had room next to each other on the floor and two had to take their places at the feet of the shorter persons. The tension grew and one night, turning over in my sleep, I accidentally hit the woman next to me in her face with my elbow. Startled by the shock, she struck back and got hold of my hair.

"What's the big idea, you brat!" she yelled.

I tried to fend her off.

"It was an accident, why would I hit you in the middle of the night?" It was dark in the room and we could barely see each other.

"Just calm down," Mother intervened, and tried to pull us apart. But Frau Armhorst was so enraged that she couldn't listen to reason. She attacked Mother, too. Then Renee felt compelled to help us, and it turned into a wild hair-pulling contest. The other women finally succeeded in breaking up the fight before the guards became aware of it.

The most embarrassing task was the use of the toilet. In the beginning, it was impossible for most of us to relieve ourselves in front of everybody. Holding up a coat as a screen gave little help.

On the other hand, since the stool was very new, we were able to rinse our underwear in it, and this kept us relatively clean. The washbasin and water pitcher were hardly adequate for our personal washing.

The days went by with unnerving slowness. There was absolutely nothing to do and the boredom was tearing on our nerves to the point of nervous breakdowns.

Frau Heimlich, one of the women from Germany, tried to cheer us up by reading our palms.

"You had a delightful childhood," she declared, holding my hand. "One little love affair, but you lost him very fast." (She had to be referring to a short romance with a German soldier who was killed on the Russian front.)

Then she continued: "You are going on a long trip."

That also was quite possible. We shouldn't be here much longer and wherever they would take us, it was probably far away. She read in our hands that we soon would be free, but when nothing happened, resentment and anger grew against her. Some of the women even went as far as to hold her responsible for them being in the prison in the first place.

Occasionally, one or the other of us was lucky enough to be called to work outside the prison. It was one way to escape the depressing surroundings of that crowded, smelly cell. Usually we were taken to cleaning in schools or offices. It was hard and degrading work in many cases, but it kept us away from the prison for a while.

One morning, the matron pointed at me to follow her. She took me to the prison garden and, together with some other women, we harvested a huge kohlrabi field. I enjoyed that thoroughly, and at the end of the day I even managed to smuggle two of the tasty tidbits in my bra back into the cell.

The highlight of our assignments undoubtedly was when Renee and I were sent together to wash dishes in the cafeteria at the YMCA. We had plenty to eat that day, from all the food left on the dirty plates!

However, at the end of the day when we were to be taken back to the prison, we made a distressing discovery. Maria Engelbrecht, the other woman from Germany, had been stripped of her clothes.

"Who did this to you?" I asked. She was close to tears, and didn't answer. Obviously, somebody had taken a liking to her beautiful things. Her trench coat, her wool skirt, the blouse, her sturdy hiking boots, even her slip, her bra and her silk panties had been exchanged for disgustingly dirty replacements. Fortunately, the prison administration had no sympathy for the thieves. After all, this was an "orderly" prison, and when the depredation was reported, the culprit was detected and forced to return the goods. Nevertheless, Frau Engelbrecht had to go through lengthy interrogations to prove that the stolen clothes were really hers.

Another time I was taken to a railroad station and handed a pail with water and scrub brush.

"Scrub the floor," I was told.

The people were indifferent and ignored me, which was just as well. I had enough abuse for a while. At lunchtime, one of the office workers shared his sandwich with me. He could have gotten into serious trouble for that, but he obviously didn't care.

"You probably won't be in that prison for very long," he assured me kindly. "You will be shipped to Germany very soon." (Was that the long trip Frau Heimlich had predicted?)

I listened to the man with mixed emotions. Why should we go to Germany? We had lived in Prague for the last eleven years; this was home for us. Yes, I was born in Germany, but I knew very little of it. We had lived in Berlin. I was seven years old when Adolf Hitler became chancellor in 1933. I vaguely remembered brown-clad men marching, singing through the streets. We heard of street fights between social democratic youths and the newly formed "Hitler *Jugend*." Then the pursuit of the Jews began and one morning the store of a Jewish furrier on our street was vandalized and the man was arrested.

Dad made a significant decision:

"We will have to leave Germany before it is too late and the same will happen to us!"

We were not Jewish, but Dad's father was, and under this new regime, that was incriminating enough. The move to Vienna, Austria was planned and put into action.

The time we spent in Vienna was a short but lovely year. Then my father accepted an engagement with the German theater in Prague and we came to this country. We had to make great adjustments, for none of us spoke the Czech language and the attitude of the Czech people toward anybody of German descent was, at times, very hostile. It happened to me many times that groups of young people followed me and called out: *"Nemka, Nemka"* – German, German. Often it became very frightening when they didn't restrain themselves to just verbal abuse but started waving sticks and throwing stones, similar to the events of the past weeks.

I entered one of the German grade schools where it was mandatory to learn the Czech language and I mastered it quite rapidly. My sister Renee went to a private British college to continue the English education she had received in Berlin and Vienna, and took Czech in night school.

Prague was the center of musical culture and I had ample opportunity to enjoy many concerts and operas as well as stage plays. Mozart became my favorite composer, and highlights like the *Noctorno* and *Eine kleine Nachtmusik* brought the most pleasant experiences into my life when played by candlelight in the courtyard of the Bertramka. This was a 17th Century villa where Mozart had spent many visits and finished his *Don Giovanni*. Other great concerts by the Prague Symphony orchestra became a frequent enjoyment, and famous conductors like Herbert von Karajan and Wilhelm Furtwaengler took the baton occasionally for guest appearances.

One performance of Shakespeare's *Much Ado About Nothing* brought me together with my first romance. A group of German soldiers from a tank division attended the play and sat in orchestra seats. My sister and I were sitting in a box on the first floor, and during the show I noticed that one of the young men kept glancing in my direction. I don't think he saw much of performance. During intermission, while having a glass of lemonade, he tried to get my attention, but obviously was too shy to speak to me. However, when we left the theater, I felt something being stuffed on the top of my muff. It was a small piece of paper.

"Please, call me sometime," read a short note. Then a name: Heinrich Dieters, and a telephone number.

"Hey, you got yourself a date," Renee giggled. "He sure is handsome," she added. "Ha, ha. My little sister is blushing!"

A few days later I worked up enough courage to make that phone call and consequently had several dates with him, until he was sent to the Russian front. He was eventually killed in battle at Stalingrad.

I had lost track of my friends during the last few years, but Prague had become home to me, and I could see no reason to leave.

But I wasn't going to argue with this man in the train depot, especially since he obviously didn't mean any personal harm.

CHAPTER SEVEN

FEATHERS AND SAUERKRAUT.

When I came back to the prison that evening, I noticed that long narrow tables had been placed in the hallway with benches on one side. Were we going to be able to eat our meager meals at a table instead of standing up or sitting on the floor? The thought appealed to me. But I was to be disappointed, for the next morning we were called out of the cell and told to sit down on the benches, but not for breakfast. One of the matrons came with a big bag of feathers, placed a small pile in front of each of us and commanded: "Strip the quills."

That was a job most of us had never done before, but we had to learn fast. And before the day was over we all had aching backs and our fingertips were tender and sore. We had to move very slowly, and there was no talking allowed. Then one of the little downs found its way into my nose, causing a vigorous sneeze that I couldn't hold back. The effect was disastrous! A soft cloud of white fluff engulfed us, feathers settled in our hair and on our clothes.

There was an element of humor in that episode, but the matron was furious, and nobody dared to laugh. She grabbed me by the hair and with a hard shove, pushed me back into the cell.

"I'll teach you to sneeze on my feathers," she yelled.

"I couldn't help it!" I cried, but my objection enraged her even more.

"You stay there till you rot!" she screamed, and slammed the door shut.

However, the next day I was allowed to join the others again and we each got a piece of cloth to put over our mouths and noses. That way other accidental sneezes were unlikely. We stripped quills for about a week, then the supply was apparently exhausted and the monotony of our days began all over again.

One other day we were moved to a different cell. The room was much larger than the one we had occupied for the last four weeks. But the size of it didn't improve the situation, for instead of twelve, there were now forty of us.

The light that could have drifted through the big barred window was blocked by a brick wall about five or six feet away. Only by stepping close to it was it possible to see the sky.

Mother, Renee and I found a spot on the floor. We spread our coats to claim the territory. There was a large sink by the door, with running water. That was an improvement. The toilet was encased with wooden boards, so there was actually some privacy. But since our number had more than tripled, we weren't much better off. There was a constant line at the toilet as well as at the sink.

In the evening, one of the women, Frau Christopher, sat on the windowsill looking up to catch a glimpse of the stars. She had tears in her eyes and after a while, the sound of her beautiful voice filled the air. She sang one of the most popular German folk songs and the melody echoed from the wall across, floated into the gray courtyard and back up into the sky.

"Ich weiss nicht, was soll es bedeuten, dass ich so traurig bin!" – I know of no reason why I should be sad. Most of us knew the lyrics and soon we joined in.

"The night is so cool and darkened, and the river flows quietly on." It was the legend of the mermaid Lorelei who sat on a rock by the Rhine River and with her singing lured passing fishermen into the deep river to their death.

Everything we felt came out with every note, but one-by-one we had to quit again as the whole misery of our situation came clearer with every tone, with every word. Tears choked our voices and instead of singing, our sobbing filled the room.

I finally cried myself to sleep and so did the others.

The next morning, we were told to take our clothes off so we could have a shower.

The thought of a bath brought back memories of our life in Vienna, when one of my parent's friends who owned a *Weinstube* on the main street of Nussdorf took advantage of our modern bathroom. Once a week this friendly chubby person came and spent at least two hours in our tub. The highlight of her visit undoubtedly came when she emerged, her face pink and shiny, her body smelling from talcum powder and laundry soap. From a huge wicker basket she would dish out mountains of cold cuts, cheese, fresh bread and of course a bottle of wine

I always looked forward to her visits, not so much for the food, but because the woman herself fascinated me. She sat at our table, her dark curly hair still damp from the bath, her pleasant round face covered with a beaming smile. When she laughed, it rang like a silver bell through the room, and her whole body wiggled. In my childish seven-year-old conception, I thought she was the greatest lady in Vienna. Perhaps it was her size that impressed me, for she was almost as wide as she was tall, and much of her hung over the edge of the chair. Often we returned her visits by patronizing her wine cellar and having dinner at her outdoor restaurant. Under shady trees, among blooming bushes, we listened to romantic *Schrammerlmusik*, a type of music one can find only in Vienna.

The "bath" we were about to receive, however, had little resemblance to the comfortable tub we offered our friend in Vienna. Dressed only in our coats, we were led through hallways and gates to the other part of the prison. The smell of food filled the air and made our mouths water. The kitchen had to be located here somewhere. The hall was lined with big barrels, and it didn't take us long to figure out that they were filled with sauerkraut.

Hungry as we were, it seemed like a welcome supplement to our diet and since there was a little delay in the line, two of us started climbing up the barrels. They were filled to the rim and it was easy to reach in and get handfuls of the tasty treat.

A half a dozen hands stretched out to us: "Give me some." "Please give me some!" We passed as much as we could to the others. A little problem was of course the storing of the stolen goodies, for though some of it was eaten immediately, it would be nice to have some later. We didn't think very long: the pockets of our coats had to do, and we stuffed the kraut in there. We also decided to stop again on the way back.

The so-called shower was a very hasty running under a line of little more than dripping showerheads. A little piece of soap was handed to us, but it really was not a good idea to use it because we hardly got a chance to rinse it off. It was hard to understand what the hurry was; we obviously weren't going to go anywhere!

On the way back we attacked the sauerkraut barrels again, only this time one of the matrons saw us. Pushing and shouting, they investigated our coats by ripping them all open, only to see a number of naked bodies underneath.

However, the loot was discovered in the pockets and all the treasures were confiscated.

But it was a good try and most of us got a taste.

Chapter Eight

Dear Lord,
Don't Let Her Die!

Except for these weekly "Express Showers" our personal hygiene was grossly neglected and there was no way that we could use the toilet in this cell to wash our underwear. We used the little piece of soap we had gotten in the shower to do our laundry in the large sink. However, there was always a long waiting line and we had to take our turns with the other thirty-seven women there, as well as at the toilet. In short, the furnishings for personal cleaning were extremely inadequate and soon we discovered the first signs of lice in our hair.

To prevent a general infestation, the prison administration provided us with lice powder and other medications. After several applications, we managed to keep the little pests pretty much away. However, something else was to make our life miserable.

Little white bugs appeared in our clothing.

Nobody knew what they were until one of the matrons, abhorred by the sight, with a disgusted expression on her face explained, "What you have there are clothes lice!" Then she declared, "The only way to get rid of them is to burn your clothes."

Since that was not possible, all we could do was kill them one by one going along the seams of our dresses and underwear, squashing the eggs and lice between our thumbnails. A grueling task indeed. It became a daily chore, but it was the only way to keep ahead of these detestable critters.

Since these lice were also carriers of intestinal diseases, the inevitable happened. Two of the older women, Frau Hagen and Frau Obermeier, both in their eighties, came down with dysentery. The only toilet in the room was constantly occupied by one or the other. To ease the situation, two pails were brought in and these poor old ladies had to sit on them – day and night. Both women had become so thin and weak that it was surprising they could sit up at all.

One night we were awakened by a strange noise. Then somebody cried out:

"Oh, my God! Oh, my God!"

At the same time the unpleasant smell that

had prevailed ever since the two women sat on their pails escalated to the point where it took my breath away. It was dark in the room, but it became frightfully clear to me that one or both pails must have tipped over.

The women closest to the door pounded their fists against it to get the guard's attention.

"Help us here, please help us!"

The light went on and there we saw one of the old women lying in a puddle of blood and excrement. She was unconscious.

"Oh, my God," Frau Krommer exclaimed again. "Oh, my God!" We were all standing in consternation around the foul mess.

"You two pick her up!" the matron finally ordered, pointing at the two women closest to her. Then the matron left and returned with a pail of soapy water, some rags and a mop, and ordered Frau Christopher and me to clean up. With a dustpan, we scooped the blood and excrement into a pail, while I was barely able to keep from throwing up. Then we mopped the rest. After it was cleaned up another matron came with a pail of hot water and disinfectant.

We begged to have the two sick women taken out before we all got whatever they had.

"All right," said one of the matrons. "We'll put them into another cell, but one of you has to go along and take care of them." She looked around. "Any volunteers?"

A breathtaking silence followed that announcement. A slight moaning from one of the sick women was all I could hear.

Then it happened.

"I'll go."

It was a small voice. One could hardly hear it, but I stood right next to her and it sounded like a trumpet to me. It was my sister who had spoken and my heart stood still.

"Oh no," Mother moaned. "Not you, please not you!"

I couldn't believe my ears or my eyes. There she was, skinny and pale, willing to save thirty-seven women from possible infection, exposing herself to certain contagion! It was an emotional but hasty goodbye, and after the three had left, the efforts of the other women to comfort Mother and me had little effect.

Six horrifying days of uncertainty and worries followed. No one would tell us how they were getting along and especially how Renee was doing.

Strangely enough, the thought never entered my mind that she might die too. When she finally came back, she was even paler and skinnier than before, and her eyes had a feverish shine.

Sure enough, she had caught it, too.

Only once before could I remember Renee being so sick that I was afraid she might die. That was when we both were children in Berlin. Mother had kept her home from school that morning because she had run a slight temperature.

When I came home and turned the corner by the dairy bar, I noticed an ambulance in front of our apartment building. For a moment my heart stood still, only to rush to my throat, and beat there like a hammer.

"Oh, maybe it's the little lady on the second floor, maybe she had a heart attack," I tried to calm myself. I started to run. A few neighbors were standing at the door.

"Who is sick?" I asked

Someone said, "I think it's your sister."

Terror struck me again. So it wasn't the little lady on the second floor after all! "Please don't let her die, oh dear God, please don't let her die!"

Renee and I had always been close. She was five years older than I, and she was the best friend a girl could have. Oh, I often resented her patronizing ways, and occasionally we had violent fist fights, but we shared our troubles and joys and most of all she protected me from the neighborhood bully and rescued me more than once from troubling situations I had gotten myself into.

Completely out of breath, I arrived on the fifth floor. Never before had I taken those steps that fast. The apartment door was open and two white-clad men carried a stretcher out. Mother came after them wearing her hat and coat, ready to go with them. "Renee will be all right," she said in her quiet voice when she saw my despair. "They will take good care of her in the hospital and make her well again. You go into the flat, and you and Dad have something to eat."

Eat! Who could eat at a time like this? I bet my mother didn't.

Renee was lying there on that stretcher, just as she was now on the dirty prison floor, her eyes closed, her face flushed from a high fever.

On the stretcher, Renee didn't even look at me when I bent over her.

"I want to go with her, please take me along!"

But Dad took me by the arm. "They don't allow children at the hospital unless they are sick," he said. "Come on in."

The medics carefully lowered the stretcher down the stairway and Dad closed the door.

"She has pneumonia, and she has to have medical care that we can't give her here. That's why she has to go to the hospital," he explained.

Then he took out one of his big white handkerchiefs and wiped my tears.

"Will she die?" I asked, still sobbing.

"Oh no, she will be fine in no time – I promise."

We went into the kitchen. Mother had started dinner and seeing the pots boiling on the stove, all of a sudden I was hungry. I was always hungry when I came home from school. Dad took a fork and tested the potatoes.

"They are done," he stated.

Then he took two potholders and drained the water over the sink. To see my father in the kitchen actually doing kitchen work was the most unusual thing I could imagine. Normally, the only time he would step into this room was to lift the pot covers to peek at what was for dinner. There were three women in house, well, two and a half, and as far as he was concerned, the kitchen was their territory.

Nevertheless, now he moved around as if he had never done anything else before and I stood there with my mouth open.

"Hey, young lady, set the table. This is not a restaurant!"

His eyes had a mischievous sparkle as he said this and then we both had to laugh. This removed some of the pressure from my chest. Sitting down to eat, my appetite came back and I was confident that Renee would be back home again, soon.

After dinner, another amazing thing happened. As I cleared the table and set the plates into the sink to be washed, Dad said, "Where are the towels? Let's surprise Mother and do the dishes."

Now, in all the six years of my life, I had never seen my Dad do dishes! He didn't even know where the towels were. And now he expected me to wash the plates so he could dry them.

Incredible!

The expression on my face brought on a hardy laugh. He knew what I was thinking.

"Come on," he exclaimed. "I know how! You will have to put them away though since I don't know where they belong."

So Dad and I spent the time together until Mother came home, doing something that we had never done together before. And my heart became lighter with every minute. I was certain that all would be well with Renee.

Oh, how I wished that he could be here with

us now, many years later with Renee so sick again. But we didn't even know where he was, or if he was still alive.

Considering her sacrificial deed, they allowed a doctor to treat Renee. He was Czech, an inmate himself because he had treated German citizens.

"Will she be all right?" was the burning question again. His answer was grave:

"The medication I will give her is very strong and depending on how her body will react, she can go either way. I can't promise you that I can save her. She is so very weak."

Her physical condition and the complete undernourishment during the past two months didn't give her much of a chance.

"Just pray for her," he suggested.

For several days she was between life and death, delirious most of the time and our prayers and tears were with her constantly. Every morning, as soon as the door was opened, the doctor rushed in to check on her, and like a miracle, the fever finally broke.

Renee was completely exhausted and had no strength left whatsoever. Her recovery went very slow even though she received bigger food rations: two small pieces of bread instead of one, two ladles of soup instead of one, and even though all of us were starving, none of the other women envied her the extra food.

At one of his visits, I approached the doctor bravely: "Sir, we were separated from our father and

I suspect that he might be in an infirmary. Do you think you could find out for us where he is? As a doctor you must have access to various sick bays."

He was very friendly: "Yes, I will see what I can do."

After a few days he was able to give us some information. Dad was in the hospital in a different prison in Prague. Of course this wasn't good news, but he was alive and God willing he would recover and we would eventually be reunited again.

Off and on Renee's recovery seemed to take a turn for the worse, and at times we thought she wasn't going to wake up at all when she had fallen asleep.

For our daily walks in the prison yard, we had to carry her the two flights of stairs. And of course, she could only sit while the rest of us marched to the *Raz-dwa-raz-dwa*, one-two-one-two of the guard.

Left, right, left, right.

Sometimes it changed to the tone of a whistle. Even though it was fresh air and some exercise, it was just as depressing as the rest of the situation. High prison walls, seven stories high, all the way around with small barred windows. Sometimes colorless faces appeared, searching eyes trying to discover a lost loved one among the marching inmates in the courtyard.

It was a hot summer and these outings, depressing as they were, were a welcome change in our monotonous existence and to a certain extent even somewhat refreshing.

We also were able to talk to some of the

matrons more often, especially to the one with the beautiful eyes who had given us our first piece of bread.

We were still determined in our search for our father, and my sister and I felt that this woman could be trusted. So we approached her like we had the doctor and she, too, agreed to help us and inquire about his condition.

CHAPTER NINE

THE LABOR CAMP.

One morning at the end of August, we were awakened before daylight.

"Get your things together," the matron instructed us.

There was really nothing to get together. All we had were the clothes on our bodies. The suitcases we had at the beginning were never returned to us. So, all we had to do was to put on our shoes and line up in the hallway.

Our young matron friend was on duty and Renee and I tried once more to inquire about our father. It was difficult to talk to her with all the other guards around, but the woman finally managed to step close to my sister. She whispered something and then she guided her eyes to the ceiling. I tried unsuccessfully to understand what she was saying.

"What did she tell you?" I urged Renee. "Please tell me!"

"I am not sure." Renee had a strange look on her face. "I didn't understand her."

"Come on, I saw her talk to you. What did she tell you? Is Dad all right?"

Now Renee had tears in her eyes.

"I don't know. She said he was at peace, whatever that means. Maybe she is lying," she added.

A matron urged us to move on, so we couldn't talk anymore. One-by-one we were checked out of the prison and for the first time in two months, we were on the street again. It was still dark and there was nobody around except us, and a group of guards like the ones we had encountered when we were first arrested in May. We were a large group of sad-looking, frightened women, pale, ragged and weak, wondering what was going to happen next.

Holding hands tightly, Mother, Renee and I tried desperately to stay together.

"Step up, step up!" a man shouted.

Forming lines of five, the group took shape and the formation started to move. I couldn't begin to guess how many there were, but it seemed like they had emptied the whole prison. The trek was two blocks long, and pushing, shouting, gun-waving men were running up and down the line. Familiar streets seemed strange and unknown to me. Of course, I had never been on the street at four o'clock in the morning before.

We crossed Wenzels Square, walked along Masaryk Avenue toward Masaryk station, the main train depot of Prague. The traffic picked up a bit, but not enough to interfere with our march or to be held up by us. We passed the main entrance to the depot to be taken to the freight station.

A train of ten or fifteen boxcars was ready for us to be loaded. Planks were put up against the open doors and, like cattle, we were driven into them. I don't know how many people fit into a freight car, but there were a lot of them, and the pushing and shoving didn't stop until we were so closely pressed together that we couldn't even move our arms. Every inch of the space was occupied. The floor was very dirty, apparently coal had been transported before, and nobody had bothered to sweep.

The big sliding door closed and the train set in motion. The cars were open on top and we could see the stars slowly fading in the coming daylight.

What might this day bring? Should this transport lead us to Germany, as the man in the depot had predicted? Were we to be free, or was there more hardship to come? Nobody knew where we were going.

On both ends of each boxcar an armed guard had taken position and yelled at us from time to time.

"Keep your heads down if you don't want them blown off!"

We could not see where we were going, but

as the sun rose, Mother whispered: "I hear birds singing! Can you smell grass?"

"We must be somewhere in the country," Renee agreed.

The sun was high. It had to be noon when the trained slowed down and eventually stopped.

The sliding doors were pushed open and I could see that we were in the middle of a field. In the distance, a church tower and houses revealed a town, but no building or shack was near us to indicate a railroad station. It was not clear to me why we stopped there.

Nevertheless, unloading began.

It was a beautiful summer day, all blue sky and sunshine, the air clear and clean. After months of stuffy air and imprisonment it felt like freedom!

In the bright daylight I could see now that the transport didn't only consist of women. Men and children poured out of the freight cars as well. My legs were asleep and so numb from the long, standing trip that I could hardly walk. And some of the people collapsed.

"You better carry them," a guard ordered. "If they can't walk they just have to lay here and die."

It was a slow march.

Our destination over a dusty road was a former Nazi concentration camp. Barbed wire, but no bars. This seemed to me like a big improvement from where we came from!

The wire was around only three sides of the camp, the fourth side bordered on a lake. Five spacious barracks and a smaller building which was the administration office were located at large distances from each other.

Registration began again. This time we each got a blanket and were assigned to one of the barracks. Women were housed in the first one, men in the second, and women with children found their bunks in the third.

The fourth barrack was the infirmary, and the largest one on top of a small hill was the kitchen and mess hall.

The blankets and the roominess were certainly improvement from the jail. We each actually had a place to sleep: bunk beds on top of each other with rough gunnysacks filled with straw. Renee and I claimed a top bunk, and mother occupied one on the bottom, next to another woman who introduced herself: "My name is Johanna Schneider. I am alone here, that is, I have no family here. You are sure lucky to be together like this!" There was a little envy in her voice, but I was sure we would be able to make friends with her.

From the long, strenuous trip and the slow march in the hot sun, we were completely exhausted and collapsed on the soft straw-filled sacks. But soon I realized that sleep was impossible. A sudden hunger pain in my stomach reminded me that we hadn't eaten since the night before and when a siren called us to the mess hall it sounded like music to my ears. The soup was similar to the soup in the prison, but it was a little thicker and had a little more taste to it. Then we were allowed to go back to our bunks to rest and recover from the strain of the trip.

Frau Schneider told us then that she had lost her husband and one of her sons on the Russian front, and that her ten-year-old daughter and her fourteen-year-old son were both separated from her during the uprising in Prague before she was brought to this camp in May. She kept saying: "Ach, you are so lucky!" And we knew that.

As soon as it got dark, she suggested to Renee and me that we stay in our bunks and pull the blankets over our heads.

"The Russians are going to come again tonight. They are looking for young girls, and when they get hold of you, you have to go with them. You know what they will do to you, don't you?"

Now I remembered that there had been Russian soldiers by the gate when we arrived. The official guard of the camp consisted of Czech militia members but apparently they had befriended some of the Russian troops, and the German girls in the camp became fair game.

However, nothing happened that night.

Tired from the excitement of the past day, we had a good night's rest on the soft straw-filled gunnysacks. For three months we had slept on the hard wood floor in the prison and now we could appreciate the change.

At dawn, a loud commotion got us up. A quick washing of our faces over one of the many sinks that lined one end of the barrack started our day. After hastily getting dressed, we marched to the mess hall for breakfast. Coffee and a piece of bread, just like in the prison. There didn't seem to be much difference in that respect. The yelling and screaming of the guards was the same, too.

Even though it was still early, the sun was already warm in the sky.

"You will go swimming now," we were told.

It didn't matter that none of us had a swimming suit.

"Just take your clothes off, and swim naked!" one of the men yelled, laughing.

Anybody who was hesitant to take off her clothes got fast help from the guards, and a wild chase toward the water began. The lake became a welcome refuge.

The guards gathered at the shore and laughingly tossed obscene remarks at us. In the excitement, I hadn't even looked at any of them. Now, from the water, I noticed that there were not only Czech guards, but also Russian soldiers.

All of a sudden it became clear to me that we didn't get this swim for our refreshment or for cleaning purposes.

These men were looking us over to decide who to get in the evening! That's why nothing happened the night before.

I froze, and for a moment the thought entered my mind never to get out of the lake, to go under and never come up again.

After a while they had seen enough, and with gunshots we were chased out of the water. Some of the bullets hit mighty close to us and it was surprising that none of the women were hit. Those men were either very good or very bad shots!

Hoping that now we could go back to the barracks and get dressed, we made a dash in that direction.

But some of the Russian soldiers tried to catch us. One of them got hold of Renee, and reached for her breasts. She screamed and kicked and slapped his hands. I jumped at him from behind, but another soldier grabbed me and guided his big hands over my nude body. I tried to ward him off by thrashing my arms and hitting his face. But he only laughed. With roaring laughter, they finally let go of us, giving us each a hard slap on our buttocks. Breathless and crying, we at last reached the barracks, and got our clothes back on.

Shortly after that, the siren sounded again from the mess hall. Frau Schneider was in front of me as we stood in line for our meal. She seemed restless, and fidgeted nervously with her food container.

"What is wrong, Frau Schneider?" I asked.

"I don't know. I have the strangest feeling," she answered, her eyes full of tears. "Something is going to happen," she went on.

"Something seems to happen around here all the time!" Mother said, trying to cheer her up.

It didn't make Frau Schneider feel any better and she received her food with trembling hands. We sat down on the narrow benches and ate the tasteless soup. Frau Schneider's hand was still shaking as she moved the spoon to her mouth.

I sat across from her, and all of a sudden all color drained from her face. Her eyes became wide in disbelief and her lips formed words that had no sound. I turned around to follow her glance and saw two youngsters standing behind me. A boy about fourteen and a girl maybe ten years old.

"Mother!" they cried in unison. "Oh, Mother!"

Frau Schneider just sat there, completely in shock.

The children ran around the table to hug and kiss her. They had arrived on the same train as we, and had roamed the camp all day in search of their mother. How fortunate they were to be united again!

Contrary to human reasoning, a spark of hope came to my mind. I exchanged looks with Renee. Could our father be here? Could we possibly find him as the Schneider kids had found their mother?

I remembered the whispering of the young matron when we left the prison.

"You never told us what the matron said to you," I pressed Renee.

"She was lying, I am sure. She said he was at peace, which probably means he is dead." I couldn't believe she could talk about it so casually.

"You mean, Dad is no more, and we will never see him again?"

"I don't know! I didn't want to believe that woman. That's why I didn't tell Mother."

Our mother had gone to the other side of the table to talk with Frau Schneider. She didn't hear our conversation and waved at us to come and join the happy group. Two of the guards came to see what the commotion was all about.

"Go back to your seats!" one of them shouted.

"I found my children, look I found my children!" Frau Schneider had gotten her speech back.

"I found my children," she kept repeating. She was delirious in her joy. "I found my Willie and my Lottie!"

Mother looked at us and I realized that she had the same hopeful thoughts that were going through my mind.

"Do you girls think we should see if Dad is here?" she whispered with a trembling voice.

"Mutti, it isn't very likely," Renee responded. "We know he was in a hospital in Prague. Please, don't build your hopes up." But Mother was determined.

"Let's look anyway!" she decided.

But our inquiries at the men's barracks and at the administration building were of no avail; there was no Victor Fuchs in the camp.

Unfortunately, we also lost a newly found friend and neighbor, for Frau Schneider was allowed to move in order to join her children in the third barracks. But we were happy for her.

This was only the second day in the camp, and already so much had happened.

The rest of the day went on with more registration. Work details were put together for the next day. The farmers of the surrounding area needed help with the harvest, and what better worker can one get than a German? The price was cheap, 15.00 Koronas a day, payable to the camp, and many farmers took advantage of the offer.

I was put into one of the detachments with eight other young people, and the next morning we walked, with two guards at our side, about eight miles to a large farm. The sun was up a while already, but in the shade of the wood the morning chill was still in the air. Walking on a narrow path, we could smell the aroma of the pine trees and mushrooms. We were not allowed to talk, and that was just fine with me. I would just as soon listen to the stillness of the tall trees, and if there were any animals to see, it was not going to happen when we made a lot of noise. Off and on something rustled in the underbrush, but whatever it was – a snake, a mouse, a little squirrel – it never came into view. At one point we came to a clearing with a little creek, and what we saw even delighted our unfeeling guards.

Our troop stopped to get a glance at a small group of deer grazing and drinking from the clear water of the stream. It lasted just a brief a moment, then the lead buck lifted his antler-crowned head, stomped his hoofs, and away they went!

Not until now did I notice that one of our guards had positioned his rifle. An ear-shattering shot rang through the quiet, but to my relief the swift animals were out of reach before the bullet could do any damage.

At the ranch we threshed all morning. Some local farmhands were working with us. Shortly before lunch I was ordered into the kitchen to help prepare food for the workers. The cooks were quite friendly and even let me have some of the carrots I was peeling. They were also interested in my personal background.

"Are you alone in the camp or do you have family there?" one wanted to know. She had a friendly smile on her round face.

"My mother and sister are there with me, but we lost our father during the uprising in Prague," I responded.

"So you lived in Prague before you came here. Were you born there?"

"No. I was born in Germany."

"You should go back there!" another woman joined in the conversation. Clearly she didn't have the same friendly attitude as the other one had, and our talk ended right there.

When the time came to break for lunch, the nourishing food became the highlight of the day. Then we went back to threshing.

Around five o'clock we got ready for the march back to the camp. As we lined up to leave, one of the cooks called me back into the kitchen and handed me an earthen pitcher full of the tasty soup that we had eaten for lunch.

"Take this home to your mother," she said. "It will do her good." I almost burst into tears. Yes, it will do Mother good, all that meat, the fresh vegetables, and the little dumplings just like she used to make herself. I could have kissed the woman, but that would have gone too far, for friendly contact with us prisoners could be a serious offense.

At that moment the guard burst into the door. "What are you doing here?" he yelled. "We have to leave, get going, you little pig!"

I almost dropped my soup. But the cook came to my defense.

"Don't get excited. I gave her some leftover soup to take home," she explained.

'To take home,' she had said. My God, have we come that far, to call that terrible camp "Home"? Were the three hard bunks with gunnysacks full of straw "Home"? The screaming guards, the swinging whips, the hunger and the misery – was that to be "Home" much longer? Of course Mother was there, and where she was, that was home, no matter how thin she had gotten and how miserable the circumstances were.

I ran out of the kitchen, holding onto the handle of the pitcher for dear life. My eyes were full of tears; I could hardly see where I was going. The pleasant day surely had taken an ugly turn.

But it wasn't over yet. The young guard kept an eye on me. He had a nasty grin on his face, and I could see he was up to no good. All of a sudden he burst out laughing.

"I know what I am going to do," he declared. "I will shoot a hole in your pitcher!" He cocked his gun and aimed at my treasured soup.

I closed my eyes and wished he would hit my legs rather than the pitcher. But nothing happened, only his laugh got louder. Apparently he had changed his mind. Hitting somebody's legs accidentally, which was highly possible since I carried the container by its handle, would surely cause him some trouble. So he resorted to just teasing me in this cruel way. However, I wasn't at all sure that he wouldn't shoot anyway, and I was trembling in fear for the rest of the hike.

The eight miles back to the camp seemed like eighty, but when I watched Mother eat the soup and felt her hugs and kisses, all ugliness was forgotten. The torture was worth the reward of knowing that she, for once, had a meal that completely filled her stomach. There was so little we could do for her. She was not young enough to be "rented out," so she had to stay in the camp and work here, moving heavy fence posts and digging ditches.

Chapter Ten

The Russians Are Coming.

The same evening after we had bedded down, when the lights were out already, the doors swung open again and a group of Russian soldiers burst into the room.

"Everybody out!" they yelled.

Helen, one of the girls, didn't climb down from her bunk right away. She was pulled down by one of the drunken intruders and pushed to the floor.

"Line up, again."

This time we were allowed to leave our clothes on.

Then they went down the line: "You come, you come and you, you come and you."

The three of us were standing trembling. Mother in the middle, clutching one of our hands on each side. When the soldiers approached us, one of them hesitated. Looking at Renee, he said something in Russian. Then he grabbed her arm and added in German: "You come, too!"

"Oh my dear God!" Mother cried. But Renee was only one of many that were taken. I didn't qualify, probably for the same reason the Militia soldiers had left me alone at my first interrogation: I was too skinny!

Mother was devastated. She trembled and cried, and I had to lead her back to her bunk. Everybody was crying. Some because they were taken, and some for joy that they were not. The lights were turned out again, and to be close to Mother I cuddled with her in her bed. Not until close to dawn did she finally fall asleep, completely exhausted.

Soon after that Renee came back. She tried not to show her anguish. She didn't speak a word and climbed immediately into her bunk, pulled the blanket over her head, and I could hear her muffled crying. She had brought a bag of food for her "service," but she couldn't eat any of it. And only because of our extreme hunger, Mother and I could accept it.

Later, Renee told us that not one, but four men had raped her. We could only hope that she would not get pregnant or worse, get a disease. Luckily, this was the only time she was caught in any of these raids, which went on almost every night. And except for the fact that she was very sore from the abuse, and could hardly walk for a few days, there were no lasting ill effects.

Some of the other women were not so fortunate. Pregnancies occurred, cases of syphilis were reported, and bad injuries were the result of multiple sexual assaults. Medical attention was mediocre, and many of the women were injured for life, if there was a life for them outside the camp ever again.

After Frau Schneider had moved to the children's quarters, a new family took her place in the bunk and the adjacent beds. Two girls, Lydia and Marlies and their mother Frau Schenk became our new neighbors. To my delight, the girls were our age and we became friends. Then, at one of the Russian intrusions, Lydia became one of their victims. She occupied the bunk next to me and one night after that she confided in me under tears that she was pregnant.

"I can't tell my mother," she whispered sobbing. "She'd kill herself."

"Maybe they can help you at the infirmary," I suggested. "You know, you are not the only one."

"I tried that. They told me I had to have the baby! What am I going to do, Elga?" She was in a state of complete despair. I didn't know what to do to help her.

On one of the next days we were placed together in a work detachment and as we walked next to each other to our destination she whispered to me: "I am going to get rid of the bastard one way or the other!"

"For God's sake, what are you going to do?" I tried to figure out what was on her mind.

"I will get rid of it, if I have to kill myself!" she burst out.

"Lydia, no!"

The following day she started bleeding, and after they took her to the sick bay she miscarried the baby. Then she developed a bad infection.

"I used a long knitting needle," she confessed, crying to her mother while we were visiting her. "Please, forgive me, Mommy!"

Frau Schenk kissed her tears away.

"Just hurry and get well again. That's the most important thing right now! I have nothing to forgive you, darling! I love you!"

But Lydia did not recover. She became one of the many casualties, and her nude body was thrown into the big hole at the far end of the campgrounds. Frau Schenk got to keep her daughter's clothing, but there was no priest or minister for any of the deaths, and the five of us, Frau Schenk, Marlies, our mother, Renee and I, were the only ones to be at the site, to say a prayer for Lydia's tormented soul. I was sure that God in His greatness would have an understanding for her action.

But where was He when the rape and the consequences happened in the first place?

Frau Schenk went into deep depression and when put into work details she functioned like a robot without any emotion or feeling. Marlies tried her best to support her mother, in spite of her own grief. And by being at her side as much as she could,

I think she prevented her mother from committing suicide.

After a few weeks, these forceful "invasions" were curbed by the commandant, and only of their free will could women be taken by the Russians. There were some who, for a meal, a can of meat, for cigarettes or just for some bread to take back to their children, went voluntarily. Yes, most of the time they were rewarded for the entertainment, but there was a bitter price to pay.

A few days after Lydia's death, I and two other young girls, Barbara and Ursula, were put into a detail to work for the Russians, and our anxiety started all over again. Mother was frantic, and I was scared to the point of panic.

But Renee kept her composure: "It is not night, Mother," she calmed us down. "Maybe they just want them to work."

Whatever it was going to be, the three of us were taken to the railroad station to unload a boxcar full of requisitioned German military supplies. The station was located only a few blocks from the camp, and when we arrived, three young, good-looking Russian soldiers greeted us with a friendly, "*Dobry jitro!*" Good morning!

The camp guard didn't stay with us this time and I thought surely he had a reason to leave us alone with the Russians.

One of the Russians spoke German and asked us if we had eaten. Since we had a piece of bread and something like coffee before we left the camp, we said yes.

"Oh, sit down anyway, we didn't eat yet. Keep us company!" was their response and we got to indulge in a feast like we hadn't had in a long time: fresh bread straight out of a farmer's oven, butter, homemade preserves, and a large glass of milk. I was still very skeptical, even after this scrumptious meal. Or was it because of it? After what happened to Renee and Lydia and all the other women, it just didn't seem to add up. They can't just be nice for no reason! But to my surprise, that was all they were, just plain nice!

We had to work hard, and carrying blankets, uniforms, clothing and guns from the train into a nearby warehouse was quite strenuous and tiresome. At noon we took a short break, and again they catered to our stomachs. This time with a thick, tasty barley soup that even had some meat in it. However, what impressed me most was that the Russians ate with us the same soup and the same bread from the big loaf we had started in the morning. We were almost too tired to go back to work after that bountiful sustenance.

Around four o'clock, we quit working and the guard came back to pick us up. As we left, the Russians gave us each a blanket and two pairs of insulated long johns. I couldn't believe that work was all we had to do for all that kindness!

"I guess they aren't all bad after all," I declared when I came back to Mother. "There are some good people left out there, and soon they will realize that it doesn't make sense to keep us here, and will let us go!"

CHAPTER ELEVEN

WHERE IS THE PERSON YOU CALL GOD?

During the four weeks we had spent in the camp so far, we became acquainted with other inmates. There were roughly one thousand of us; hundreds were children. The hardship and starvation among these little ones was more devastating than our own despair.

The children's sad-looking eyes, their constant cry for food, and their swollen bellies were witnesses to their suffering since May. Many of them had already found their freedom in the mass grave where Lydia was buried.

My mother went to the children's barracks as often as she could, and since she had nothing to give, she tried to make life a little better by singing with them and having story-telling hours.

The young mothers were also just shadows of themselves for most of them shared their meager rations with their youngsters. When the women were sent to work outside the camp, they were occasionally able to bring small food supplements from a compassionate employer, just like I had gotten the soup from the farmer's lady on one of the first days. These charitable donations made it possible for many to survive.

On one of my mother's missions I accompanied her. There I found a former classmate, Gerlinde Mahler.

"Elga," she cried when she saw me, and we fell into each other's arms. Between laughing and crying we remembered our school days. The mutual friends and the teachers came to mind.

"Do you remember Professor Weiler, the math teacher, how he pronounced Geometry?" Gerlinde asked, and then she mocked the man's word: "Gh-e-ometre-e-e-a."

"Oh yes," I laughed, and went on. "And Mister Wellinger, the art teacher. How handsome he was! Remember, we all had a crush on him!"

Gerlinde giggled. "Ya, but nobody as bad as Veronica. She almost killed herself when he got married, but not to her!"

"Poor Veronica. But she got over it. Didn't she marry a Navy officer?"

"Yes," Gerlinde replied. "And she had a darling little girl she named Dolly. That's English, you know. Because she looked like a China doll."

"What became of her?" I wondered. I had lost track of most of the girls.

"I don't know, Gerlinde answered. "But did you know that Leonora was drafted into an anti-aircraft unit and was killed in an air raid in Dresden?"

"Oh, No!" I was shocked. My dear Leonora! She and I had been best friends during the last three years of school. Her father was head custodian at the Charles University and many times I visited her in her parent's apartment there. It was a wonderful old, impressive building and I hoped that one day I might become a student in those traditional halls of wisdom. One of the reasons I loved Leonora so much was her beautiful piano playing. I could sit for hours and listen to her performances when she brought Mozart or Beethoven to life with her music. Now I had to find out that this terrible war had claimed her as one of its victims. My chest felt like a heavy rock had settled on it.

"Elga," Gerlinde interrupted my thoughts and took my arm. "I have two babies. I married too, instead of following the draft when we were all recruited in 1943. I married an SS-man." She guided me to her bunk.

"This is Juergen and this is Kurt," she presented two children. "They are twins."

Both of them were lying quietly on their bed.

I wanted to say something nice like, 'they are

beautiful,' but I couldn't because they looked as pathetic as all the other pitiable children. I picked one up. There was hardly any weight to him, and when his spindly little arms curved around my neck, I burst into tears again.

"You poor things, oh you poor little things!"

Gerlinde put her arms around the other little boy. "What will become of us? Will my children be able to live through this? Sometimes I wish they would die, rather than suffer like this!"

I knew she didn't mean that, but I could understand her feelings. And again I saw myself helplessly confronted with a situation that I could do nothing about.

"Do you know where your husband is?"

"Ach, Elga," she started crying again. "I had the shortest marriage anybody ever had. Gerhard was sent into combat two weeks after we were married and was killed a year ago. He never saw his children."

How tragic! I held her in my arms, thinking how fortunate I was compared to her. Maybe Dad was right after all when he said that nothing can be so bad that it couldn't be worse!

"Where are your parents? Did you live with them while your Gerhard was gone?"

"Yes, I did, and they were wonderful and supportive. But they were arrested first and I have no idea what happened to them."

"God willing, you will find them again." I tried to console her but since she had married an SS-man, she probably didn't put a lot of faith into God's will.

"You see, we were separated from our father, but I still hope we will find him some day," I continued.

She gave me a faint smile.

"Yes, perhaps," she replied. But there was doubt in her voice. We walked toward the door together and I promised to come back again.

"I will try to get some milk for your boys on my next assignment," I said, and a spark of hope came into her eyes.

On my way out, I stopped at the area where Mother had gathered a group of five- and six-year-olds. She told them the story of a lovely princess who was kept prisoner by a bad witch in a high tower. In order to receive her Prince Charming she let her long hair out of the window and he climbed up to visit with her. (A pretty ridiculous story actually!)

Why were these children here? What were they punished for? Was there anybody here I could talk to, and get answers to my questions? I didn't want to burden Mother, but I found somebody else.

A young man in his thirties had befriended me. With little gifts, he had appeared in our barrack and had asked if he could try to make my life a little more bearable. A piece of bread, a handful of potatoes, a couple of eggs, were among the things he had organized. How he attained them I didn't know and didn't ask.

I found Bruno in the men's barracks. We walked over the camp ground together and I had a good cry while he held my hand and listened to my lament. Why are we here? What had we done to go through this ordeal? Why were Gerlinde and her little boys and all the other innocent children held here, and starved to death? Why? Why? Who was this God who let this happen?

We sat in the grass by the lake. I had worked myself into a frenzy with my distress and cried bitterly.

"Don't cry, my little Elga," Bruno whispered. "Don't cry."

He stroked my head and I leaned on his broad shoulder.

"This tragedy will end some day and we will be free again!"

"But when Bruno, when?"

His words seemed so empty and hopeless, so meaningless and insignificant! But gradually I regained my composure and settled down. I was thankful that he had listened to me and was glad that I had poured my heart out to him.

All of a sudden I heard Bruno swear.

"Damn!" he said.

I looked up and saw a guard standing in front of us.

"What are you doing here?" he yelled, pointing his rifle at Bruno. "Don't you have better things to do, than to make love here in broad daylight?"

We scrambled to our feet. I stumbled and tripped in the excitement.

"Move, get going you little pig!"

There it was again! – You little pig.

Couldn't they find a different title for once? Oh, how I wanted to yell back, and tell him what I felt. All my apprehension that had subsided sitting by the lake came back and blind hatred overcame me. But I had learned to control myself and obediently I hurried back to our quarters, while gritting my teeth and clenching my fists. Behind me I heard the guard shouting at Bruno, and turning back I saw my friend stumbling to the ground.

"Get up, you pig," the man shouted again, and pounded the butt of his gun on Bruno's body.

'Dear God, how can he get up when this man keeps him down with his beating?' I felt like crying out but I could not help my friend and he finally staggered back to his barracks.

Back at the women's barracks, one of the younger women was in complete hysterics. She screamed and kicked and beat her fists at the floor. Her mother and some of the other women tried to calm her down, and one of them finally dumped a pail of water over her head. That settled the matter fast! The mother, Frau Sudermann and her daughters Uta and Sieglinde had their beds several bunks down the lane. Sieglinde was the one who threw the tantrum. It didn't really surprise me that she would put on such a show, whatever the reason.

When I first met them I could not imagine how they could possibly have survived the hardship and harassments in the camp for four months already. These girls were both the most pampered, finicky, spoiled and selfish individuals I had ever seen!

"This soup tastes disgusting," Sieglinde would whine. "I can't eat this! And the bread is stale and moldy."

Well, I knew that, we all did. And we had eaten stale and moldy bread since May. I wondered why she hadn't gotten used to it by now.

"Maybe you should forget about eating altogether, if nothing pleases you!"

I was angry when one day she sat next to me in the mess hall and started her complaining again.

"Your sniveling is getting on my nerves! We all feel that way, but it doesn't help to dwell on it, and it surely doesn't make the soup taste any better! If you want to survive, you better plug your nose and swallow that disgusting stuff!"

That day her hysteric outburst was brought on by envy at her sister because it seemed to her that their mother had given a larger piece of meat to Uta.

Frau Sudermann was a seamstress and had established herself quite well in the village. Her work assignments fit her trade and that's how she managed to provide her girls with plenty of food, so they actually could afford to be finicky. She even received cash money so they could buy what else they needed on the black market.

Uta and Sieglinde were put into work detachments of course, like the rest of us, but somehow they always ended up with light housework. Uta told me that once she had to work on a farm and when told to clean the barn she became so sick to her stomach that she had to throw up.

'That's pretty smart,' I thought to myself.

She didn't tell me though if she was forced to clean the barn anyway. Then I remembered the sickening incident with the tipped-over pail in the prison. That would have been quite a test for her!

At any rate, I sure didn't have much in common with these ladies and tried to avoid their company as much as I could.

CHAPTER TWELVE

THE SAD NEWS.

Somehow the situation turned a little better for us when Mother was ordered to work in the kitchen. That meant she didn't have to move heavy posts and proved to be rather beneficial in the food department.

The provisions she obtained weren't overwhelming, but they helped reduce the constant hunger for she was able to sneak us extra food rations. Unfortunately, this didn't last very long.

One day a Russian officer requested thirty-five workers to repair a road.

"I also need a cook to fix their meals," he demanded, and picked Mother for the job.

The thirty-five men were loaded into a truck and Mother sat with the driver in the cab. The officer and his driver had a jeep for their transportation. When Mother came back that night she had the most exciting story to tell.

"Girls," she started. "You wouldn't believe the frightening ride I had with this crazy Russian."

"Tell us, Mutti."

"First, he drove quite decently, but all of a sudden he stepped on the gas pedal as if it had to be punished for something, and drove so fast I thought the guys in the back of the truck would be thrown off. The speedometer went all the way up to 100 kilometers, and I didn't know where to hold on so I wouldn't fall off my seat."

"That is a bumpy dirt road, how could he go so fast?" I had walked that way many mornings, and knew it was everything but a racetrack.

"Well, Elgi, he did. And he had a lot of fun doing it!"

"You must have been scared!"

"Scared? I was petrified! But I realized that was exactly what he expected. He wanted to scare me! So I tried not to show it, and when he turned his grinning face to see my reaction, I burst out laughing. I am sure it must have sounded hysterical because I was much closer to tears than to laughter. And to show him that I wasn't scared I said, '*dobre, dobre.*'"

I interrupted her: "You mean you actually told him it was good what he did?"

"Yes, and it worked!"

"What do you mean, it worked? Didn't he get mad?"

"I think he was disappointed that I spoiled his fun by going along with his nonsense. Anyway, he slowed down."

"What happened then?" Renee wanted to know. And she added hesitantly," They didn't rape you?"

"No," Mother replied, and took my sister in her arms. She must have felt, as I did, that the recollection of her traumatic experience must have gone through Renee's mind.

"No, they didn't rape me, darling. Actually, they were quite friendly and polite, especially the officer who got me."

"Tell us more," I demanded.

"I was ordered into a tent equipped with a requisitioned German field kitchen. There were plenty of food supplies to prepare good meals for the workers, and I think they all liked my cooking. Even the Russians."

Then she had a big surprise for us. She had brought a big pot of the stew she had cooked. Not just a thin runny soup, but a solid stew with meat and potatoes and carrots, cabbage and celery. It was the highlight of the evening! It was heaven! I ate so hastily that Mother had to caution: "Don't eat so fast or you will get a stomach ache." She smiled as she said it.

She stayed with that assignment for two weeks, then the road was repaired. Every evening she brought that pot full of food for us.

"Did your outrageous driver repeat his stunt again?" I asked one night.

"Oh, yes, he tries it off and on, but I am kind of used to it and don't get scared anymore. So he doesn't enjoy it as much as he probably would like to and is giving up on it."

After that job, she was put into kitchen duty in the camp again.

*****

We now were in the second half of September. The nights started to grow longer, the days shorter. The trees put on their colorful attire and the dandelion leaves that we had gathered for salads during the summer became scarce. With concern we looked at the coming months. Were we going to be in the camp during the winter? Life here was hard to bear in the summer, what was winter going to be like?

There were only three little potbellied stoves in the whole barrack, not enough to keep the whole area warm. The windows and walls were not insulated and we could already feel the chill and draft during the nights.

Fall in Europe is damp and nasty with heavy rain at times. Flu season. Many inmates became ill and I caught a bad case of it, too. I was taken to the infirmary with a high fever. There I discovered another former classmate, Inge West. She had befriended one of the doctors and held a position as nurse.

"Oh, Inge, will you help me, please?" I pleaded in my delirium.

I am not sure if I got any special treatment from her, but Bruno came several times and once he even had a bowl of real chicken soup he had acquired from his farmer especially for me. Mother was also able to supply me with food from her kitchen job as often as she visited me.

One morning when she came, I could see that something was wrong. Obviously she had been crying again, and for the first time since Renee's illness in the prison I saw her discouraged and depressed. She had gotten very thin, just like the rest of us, and she seemed much smaller than she had been. Her hands were rough from the hard work and she didn't walk as erect as she used to. Her face had gotten wrinkled and old. Only her dark brown eyes hadn't lost their fire and spirit. The faith and the vitality she displayed in spite of the hardships she endured had helped us bear the torments of the past five months.

But that morning all her vigor seemed to have left her. She sat at the edge of my bed, holding my hand, looking at me without seeing me. Her eyes were dull, as dull as Dad's eyes had been when I saw him for the last time.

"What's wrong, Mutti?"

For the longest time there was no reaction. She just sat there, looking at me with no look in her eyes. There was no life in her. She was pale and her hands felt like ice.

When her lips finally formed an answer, it

was as if she had rehearsed the words. With no expression she spoke, and it sounded like a recording. "The commandant called me into the office this morning and told me that your father died a natural death in the prison of Panrac in Prague, in July."

After a small pause, to gather more strength, she added – and now her voice was so choked by tears that I could hardly hear her: "He is buried in a mass grave!"

It took me a while to understand what she just said. And before I could say anything, she broke down. Hearing herself giving the bad news to me brought her back to reality and made her realize the cruel truth. She sobbed bitterly, and rested her head on my bed.

"Oh, Mutti, at least he didn't suffer very long!" I tried to comfort her while my heart hurt as if someone was pulling it out of my chest. Then I remembered Renee's words quoting the young matron in the prison: 'She said he is at peace, which probably means he is dead!'

So the woman had not been lying after all, and the ominous feeling after my last meeting with Dad turned out to be right. But now that my suspicion was confirmed, I was unable to accept it. No more cozy dishwashing sessions? No more invigorating bike rides the four of us used to take to the outskirts of Prague, topped by enjoyable picnics under whispering birch trees? No more often frustrating drama lessons? No more joined theater and concert visits?

Was it all over?

It was now almost five months that we had been separated from him but he seemed to be with me all the time. I could not imagine my life without my father and a dark emptiness moved into my heart.

Still feverish and weak from my bout with the flu, I sat up, trembling, and put my arms around Mother. This wonderful, strong woman who in her quiet way had always been the backbone of our little family, who always knew the right word to say at the right time, now leaned on my chest wailing and completely dissolved in tears.

"What use is it now, to live anymore! We will never see him again. We can't even go to his grave. And we will rot here until we are dead, too!"

That was not like Mother at all, and I felt desperate and helpless. My eyes were dry and hot, but no tears came to cool them. Why could I not cry? With all the crying I had done during the past months, didn't I have any tears left? Now, when I needed it most, why could I not cry? With my emotions churning inside me, I wanted to scream and shout, but instead I held Mother in my arms, rocked her and said softly, "Don't despair, Mutti! Be happy for him that he didn't have to suffer any longer. We still have each other. We just have to stick it out here. There will be an end to this, you'll see! They can't keep us here forever."

But whatever I said, I could not get through to her. To make matters worse, Renee was not in the camp at the time. She was assigned to a permanent job and came back only occasionally to visit.

It took a long time and a lot of convincing to keep Mother from giving up. Even after Renee came back and made Mother understand that we needed her more now than ever before, she never was quite the spirited and vital woman she used to be.

CHAPTER THIRTEEN

DESPERATION.

As soon as I recovered and was back on my feet, although still shaky and weak, strengthless and undernourished, it was 'back to work.' The potato and sugar beet harvest was in full swing and every hand was needed. I wondered how the farmers of the area had brought their crops in before the German slaves were available. Did they use the Jews that occupied this camp before we came? What an irony!

The population at our camp had dwindled. Many were buried in the grave on the south end, a large number were about to die, and some had been released. Among those released were sixteen German-speaking Jews who had been caught in the web of denunciation because of their native tongue.

Every available person was put to work, and our detail was led by three guards to a large farm.

An intimidating supervisor ordered us into a sugar beet field and emphasized his demands with a large bullwhip, driving us on with shouts and curses like a herd of cattle.

There were other helpers on the premises. A group of girls whose hair had been cut like the Czech women in the prison were there on a "permanent" basis. They had their quarters in the hayloft above the barn. I was able to talk to one of them while lifting the beets out of the ground into a wagon.

"We have been here since May," she told me.

"You all seem to be about the same age. Were you all together when you were arrested?" I wondered.

Her answer came very hesitantly.

"We are former Hitler *Jugend* leaders," she whispered.

"My God!" I exclaimed. "You are lucky they didn't shoot you!"

"I don't know about the lucky part. Sometimes I wondered during the past six months. With the Russians raping most of us almost every night and this cruel overseer making our lives as miserable as he possibly can, perhaps it might have been better if we had been killed right away!"

The supervisor paraded past giving us an inquiring look and cracking his whip threateningly over our heads. The girl next to me ducked like a beaten dog and started crying nervously. At the same time she increased the pace of her moves to a hectic tempo. What must these young women have gone through!

"Three of us tried to escape once," she whispered to me softly after the man had passed. "This man beat us almost to death when they caught us." Then she showed me four barely healed scars on her back that the whip had caused.

I remembered similar treatment in the camp when some inmates had tried to run away. The beating there had been just as severe, and to inflict some torture for good measure, the guards had sprinkled salt into the open sores. The whole camp population was forced to watch the punishments as a deterrent to other attempts to escape.

For many nights I had nightmares, and the screams of the tormented men were ringing in my ears for weeks.

I looked with pity at the young girl. She was about my age and the hard work she must have done during the past few months had left obvious marks on her person. She was pale and thin, and her hands were rough and dirty. But actually, I wasn't really much better off.

The sugar beets were heavy. Each one of them was about the size of a child's head, and to pick them up after the plow had loosened them out of the ground was a backbreaking hard job. Especially in my weakened condition. It also seemed that the man had to fill some kind of quota, for none of us was able to work fast enough to please him. Shouting and cursing, he ran up and down the side of the field, spurring us on with the cracking of his whip. The guards who had stayed with us supported him with shouts and gunshots.

A short lunch break interrupted the laborious morning. We each got three potatoes, boiled in their jackets. They were hardly washed and gray inside, but it was all we got, and greedily we devoured them, dirty skin and all.

Then it was back to work again. The beets had been brought into the barnyard and unloading began. Long boards were put on sawhorses, and with large butcher knives, six of us had to cut the tops off. I looked at the knife in my hand.

'What a weapon,' I thought. There were only four of them and about twenty of us men and women. Six of us had knives! On the other side of the board, Herr Gruber looked up and I could see that his thoughts were similar to mine. He was a man in his sixties, and must have been a stately person at one time. But the hardships of the past six months had taken their toll on his posture. His eyes were deep in their sockets, his pale cheeks were thin and the skin was like parchment paper, stretched tightly over his pale face.

As he looked at me, his eyes had a strong fire and a sudden panic came to my heart.

"Oh, no. You wouldn't really…" I whispered.

I detected a slight nod of his head and with a fast motion he swung around and thrust the knife at the supervisor who, at that moment, stood cursing behind him.

It all went so fast that I couldn't quite conceive what was happening. Blood was running from the man's arm and he dropped his whip.

"You dirty pig!" he yelled, and tried to wrestle the knife from Herr Gruber's hand with his uninjured arm. Herr Gruber seemed to develop unbelievable strength and stabbed at the supervisor again and again. Then a loud gunshot rang through the air. One of the guards came to the supervisor's aid and shot Herr Gruber in the head.

An outcry of terror and fear followed the gunshot like an echo. The guards pointed their cocked rifles at us. I dropped my knife and raised my arms over my head, as did the others. The supervisor rushed cursing into the farm building, holding his wounded arm with his other hand.

I looked at Herr Gruber. He was lying in a puddle of blood, his head shattered, pieces of his skull scattered in the dirt. The sight was unbearable. I had to turn away and one of the women sank to the ground, fainting. For a moment, I thought they were going to shoot us all, the way they were waving their rifles and drove us to line up by the manure pit.

After a while, the supervisor returned to our group, his arm bandaged in a sling.

"I don't want any of these murderous German pigs on my farm anymore," he shouted. "Take them back to the camp and shoot them all!" And with his uninjured arm, he started pushing the men and women closest to him. We were chased back to the camp, running the whole way.

"I can't run anymore; my side hurts like crazy," Hilda panted next to me. And she slowed down. Her legs gave in and she fell. I tried to help her up, and one of the guards came shouting to see what the delay was.

"She can't run anymore, please let us rest a while," I pleaded. Some of the other men and women had sat down on the ground, too.

"If they want to shoot us they might as well do it right here, right now!" one of the men called out. So we actually had the chance to rest for a short time. Then the chase started all over again.

At the camp, we were told to wait in front of the administration building. The commandant came out and, looking at us, he beat his horsewhip threateningly against his boots.

I hear you people can't be trusted with knives," he started. "Well, that's too bad, you murderous bunch! To teach you a lesson I could have you all shot. Unfortunately, we need you to work for our farmers so I have to spare you 'til the harvest is in. For today you are confined to your barracks until I think of a proper punishment!"

I walked to our quarters. Mother was still in the kitchen, and Renee was not due to return from her work assignment until later in the evening. I climbed into my bunk, buried my face in the straw and started crying. I tried to block the dreadful vision of Herr Gruber's shattered head from my mind, and with repulsion I recalled how the guards had taken his lifeless body and thrown it into the manure pit.

Was that all our lives were worth now? To be thrown into manure pits and mass graves? There I was again with my bitterness, my woe, my questioning. Why? Why? And when will it end? Why don't they get it over with and shoot us right now?

Frau Unger, who had occupied a bunk on the other side, had acquired syphilis during one of the rapes and as a response had cut her wrists and bled to death two weeks ago. Was that the solution? But circumstances were different with me. I had Mother and Renee at my side. I had been spared from the frequent rapes and except for occasional beatings and the constant gnawing hunger pain, I was relatively well off compared to others. So what are you complaining about, little Elga? It could be worse, maybe not much, but it could be worse!

My tears subsided when Mother came back. She had heard what happened at the farm and since our group was excluded from our scanty evening meal, she brought me a piece of bread. Her presence gave me strength again. And when Renee joined us later, we cuddled together on Mother's bunk and again found comfort in each other's company as we had found it before in the prison in Prague.

CHAPTER FOURTEEN

WINTER STORMS
AND CHRISTMAS.

On November 2nd, the first snow announced the approach of an early winter. It was not just scattered flakes that soon would be absorbed by the sun. There was enough snow to produce a thin white layer on the fields and roads. The temperature dropped considerably and our clothing left a lot to be desired.

The long johns the Russian soldiers had given to me were a welcome supplement. Since they were way too big for me, I was able to pull part of them all the way over my chest. To hold them up, I fastened them with a string and tucked the leggings over my feet into the wooden shoes which we received after our own had fallen apart. It was difficult to walk that way, but it kept most of the cold from reaching my bare toes. However, since I owned only the skirt I wore since we had been arrested, I portrayed quite a ridiculous sight. When I arrived at my assigned farm that morning, the farmer's lady took one look at me, beckoned me into the house and outfitted me with a pair of slacks.

"You can't run around in such an indecent getup," she decided. But all I was interested in was that I was considerably warmer with these ugly long johns than without them. Nevertheless, the added cover of my "new" slacks felt twice as warm and I gratefully accepted it.

The day had started gray and dreary, and threatening clouds were hanging full of snow in the gloomy sky. We were in the field, gathering potatoes. My fingers were cold and sticky from the moist dirt, but the guard, wrapped in his warm fur-lined coat, had no compassion when I tried to scrape the mud from my hands. As far as he was concerned, I wasted too much time cleaning my hands and he was eager for us to get done with the work. Finally, this day came to an end and we started our march back to the camp.

Somebody had started a fire in one of the little potbelly stoves and a number of women were clustered around it. There was some firewood lying around on the camp grounds, and we were allowed to collect as much as we could find. However, the little stoves gave only enough heat to keep just the immediate area around them warm. A few feet further away it was bitter cold and the drafts from the doors and windows made our suffering even more unbearable.

Additional snow covered the ground, the lake froze, and there were only occasional work assignments to fill, so the additional food supplies dwindled significantly. Many inmates suffered frostbite, which turned into ugly boils in some cases and it seemed as if people just withered away.

On one of my visits with Gerlinde, I found her sitting on her bed. A couple of times I had been able to keep my promise, and had acquired a little milk for her babies. She sat motionless, holding one of the twins tightly in her arms, while the other one was lying at her side. His big eyes were wide open and appeared even bigger in his thin face as he reached for me with his bony little hands. I picked him up and looked at his mother. There was a distant look in her face. Then she started rocking the child, and hummed a lullaby.

"Sleep, sleep my precious prince."

I put Juergen down and tried to take Kurt from her embrace. He was dead.

"He died in his sleep. He is not hungry anymore." There were no tears, Gerlinde couldn't cry anymore. I put my arms around her.

"You still have Juergen," I whispered.

"I know," she said. "I know."

She let go of the dead child. I wrapped him in his small blanket and we took his lifeless little body to the South corner of the camp to join Lydia and all the others who didn't make it. Gerlinde carefully lowered her precious little load down the side into the pit. She knelt on the ground, took a handful of the wet snow and dropped it.

"What a burial," she whispered; scraping more snow together, trying to cover the small shape below.

Suddenly she cried out: "Why is this happening to us? What did my Kurt do, to be so miserable and die so young?"

I had the same questions on my mind – many times. I handed Juergen to her without a word and she eagerly clutched him in her embrace.

"Just don't you die on me, too. Please, Lord, let me keep him!"

That was quite a switch for her to call on the Lord, for her upbringing and her marriage to an SS-man were far from being religious. But I could understand her feelings. It was as if she was trying to count the one blessing she had left and she wanted to cling to it.

I looked at my own situation. I had Mother and Renee, and again I felt strengthened and optimistic about the fact that we were still together. My father's death had left a tremendous vacuum in my life, but when I witnessed the hardships, the tortures and the maltreatments the men at the camp were going through, I could only repeat to myself: 'Thank you, Lord, that Dad didn't have to suffer longer than he did!'

Gerlinde and I walked back to the barracks. She held on to Juergen so tightly that the child started to cry.

"Oh, my dear little one. I just don't want to lose you! I didn't mean to hurt you!" She kissed him lovingly.

I hated to leave my friend alone, but I had to go back to our place and she seemed pretty much in control of her feelings, so I gave her one more supporting hug and she returned to her quarters.

It started to snow again and an icy wind blew the flakes around in little whirlpools. I pulled the hood of my coat over my head and buried my hands in my pockets. Shivering, I reached our quarters and there I found my sister sitting on Mother's bunk. Her left arm was bandaged.

"Oh dear, what happened?"

She was pale and her hands were ice cold.

"I had to leave my farmer because I developed a big boil on my arm," she explained. "Where were you? We were looking all over for you."

I told her about Gerlinde's child and she had tears in her eyes when she said, "How many more of those little ones will have to die?"

She was in pain, for the doctor had drained her abscess without any kind of anesthesia.

"Please get Mother," she pleaded.

I ran to the kitchen and Mother got permission to leave when I told the chef what happened. Then I hurried to the infirmary. I was determined to get some pain pills for Renee. Inge West, my former classmate, managed to sneak me a couple of aspirins. Why couldn't they give Renee something to ease her pain in the first place? It made me angry that these people who called themselves doctors, and were prisoners too, would actually torture their fellow inmates!

The snow had increased and the wind was howling around the barracks when I finally came back. Renee tried not to show her pain but she gratefully swallowed the pills. After a while she fell asleep on Mother's bunk.

The next morning, both of her arms and her hands showed a slight swelling.

"I have no feeling in my fingers," she declared.

We took her back to the sick bay, fearing she might have blood poisoning. But the doctor diagnosed it as a nerve infection – and did nothing about it.

"It will go away," he stated.

But it didn't. It became worse. Her lower arms and her hands became practically paralyzed. We had to clothe and feed her, tension mounted and at times she would get very irritable and impatient.

"Why in the world does everything have to happen to me?" she would exclaim. "Can't I be as lucky as you for once?"

I would have gladly taken some of her misfortune, but all I could do was to try to help her as much as I could.

To make matters worse, we were unable to keep ourselves and our clothing as clean as we did when the lake was open, and lice and fleas started to make our lives miserable again. When one day one of these little pests rested peacefully on Renee's chest and she couldn't catch it, she went into hysterics.

"Catch it! Catch it! For God's sake catch that lousy thing!" she screamed.

But by the time I got there the flea had jumped away and then all hell broke lose.

"Why can't you help me?" she snapped at me. "You have two good hands, can't you even catch a flea?"

It isn't always easy to catch a flea, even with two good hands. Those little critters are quite fast, and many times – now you see them, now you don't. And only the traces of painfully itching marks are witnesses of their presence.

But at that point my sister had lost all sense of reasoning. She jumped up from the bunk and with her arms in the air she ran screaming through the barrack.

"Help me, somebody help me," she yelled.

She ran to the door and since she could not open it with her hands, she started beating her fists against it and kicking it with her feet. It went so fast, and her outburst caught us all by surprise, that we were too late to prevent her from breaking the windowpane in the door. By that time one of the guards got a hold of her and with one blow of his gun, struck her to the ground. Blood ran from her head onto the snow and I was sure he had killed her. Mother and I rushed to see what the man had done.

"Not she too, oh please, not she too! I just lost my husband! Dear Lord, don't let her die, too!"

Mother was desperate as she knelt by Renee's side. Another hit with the gun put a fast end to

Mother's crying. As she was lying on the ground and I was trying to tend to her, two other guards came and carried Renee to the infirmary. She was not dead, but the cut in her head required a number of stitches.

She recovered after several days from that injury, but her hands were immobile for a long time. They finally decided to give her vitamin shots, and slowly Renee got better.

But the misery and the dying went on. The big hole at the south end of the camp was used more and more. The bodies were stripped of their clothing, for there was great need for any available cover against the cold and the dead didn't need their clothing anymore.

Often I thought that our father was in a hole like that and I wondered if he was without clothes too, or if perhaps in a city like Prague they did things differently.

We worried very much for Mother, for she had gotten so thin and looked almost transparent. She became weak and seemed to be fading away. We secretly shared our rations with her but she found out and got angry with us.

"This is little enough. You eat your own food," she insisted.

*****

Christmas came.

Our spirits seemed broken. Nobody cared anymore. To celebrate, our usual potato soup was replaced by barley soup with some horsemeat in it. And an added bonus – maggots.

At this point that didn't even bother us anymore. As disgusting as it was, we just fished the yellow worms out and ate the soup.

Someone had gotten a candle. It represented a Christmas tree.

"Silent night, Holy night."

I tried to sing, and some of the others attempted to join me, but the song chocked on our tears.

Looking at each other, and holding hands, I thought of our father bringing in a Christmas tree the afternoon of Christmas Eve. He carried it secretly, as secretly as one can carry a tree into the living room, locking the door behind himself.

Renee and I busied ourselves finishing gifts and helping Mother get dinner ready: traditional carp, and brown beer gravy with raisins and pears in it. The fish had been purchased alive a few days before, and swam in the bathtub until Dad butchered it in the morning.

There was a wonderful smell all through the apartment from sweet bread, cookies and good food. To make it smell even more like Christmas, Mother had burned some pine branches, and the incense-like odor filled the air with a sweet aroma.

When dinner was ready, Dad came out.

"The tree is decorated and now we have to wait for the Christ child. Let's eat dinner. I am hungry," he said.

In spite of the excitement and the anticipation, dinner was always wonderful and even though I thought I couldn't eat a bite, I always cleaned my plate.

When finally the little silver bell announced the arrival of the Christ child, and the open door revealed the sparkling Christmas tree, the greatest wonder of my childhood repeated itself year after year.

Later, Dad told me once that he enjoyed these Christmas surprises as much as we did, and that he often wondered what sparkled more, the Christmas tree or our eyes.

I heard a little sob. Mother had leaned her head against Renee's shoulder and tears ran down her thin face.

Had the Lord forgotten us? Why did we have to spend this most joyous day under such depressing circumstances?

We had lost all hope – did we lose faith too?

CHAPTER FIFTEEN

NEW YEAR'S EVE.

The mood in the camp had fallen to a depressing low.

People were moping around, yearning for something to do. There was little demand for workers. Who would have thought that the hard labor we were exposed to during the summer would appear to be appreciated now? Some of the men were "lucky" to be ordered to do some snow shoveling in the village and in the camp, but for most of the inmates, boredom became an agonizing experience.

To break the monotony and boost the morale, somebody in the men's barracks came up with the idea of having a New Year's party.

Permission was given by the commandant. A poster on the bulletin board in the mess hall asked for volunteers for a talent show. The response was far from enthusiastic.

"To put on a talent show is ludicrous. We have no music or props!" Frau Heilmeier stated. "And who wants to party anyway?"

However, several people did sign up, reluctantly at first, to sing, put on skits and little theater scenes and to everybody's surprise, all kinds of hidden talents were discovered. Frau Schulte demonstrated an amazing tap dance. And Herr Sodermann and his wife sang a duet.

There was plenty of time for rehearsal, and little by little, more men and women became eager to participate.

A spark of my theatrical background lightened the gloomy situation for me. I knew it was not going to be like the times when I participated in Dad's radio shows in Prague or studied Julia's part from *Romeo and Juliet*, or Gretchen from *Dr. Faust* under my father's direction.

I had always loved Gretchen's plea to the Virgin Mary:
"Oh bend thou, mother of sorrow,
send thou a look of pity on my pain."
The plea could easily relate to our suffering here, even though it had a completely different meaning in the drama. So I decided to make the entire prayer my contribution to the show.

However, despite that it was probably a good performance – or because of it – the audience reacted with sadness and tears.

Berta and Susi sat there holding on tightly to each other, shedding bitter tears and some of the older women sobbed openly. Even some men had tears in their eyes. Of course this did not contribute one bit to the uplifting of their spirits.

On a lighter note I sang *"Three sails in the sunset"* together with Bruno later in the program. Renee was in a couple of humorous skits and had a good round of applause. The display of these and other talents brought a little enjoyment into our unpleasant lives.

Before the show, which was held in the mess hall, we were given a "festive meal" in the form of barley soup with pieces of horsemeat like on Christmas Eve. This time there were no maggots in it. I thought of the wonderful meals Mother would prepare on New Year's Eve. It was usually a pork roast to bring prosperity in the coming year.

When I was a little girl I always thought that at midnight on New Year's Eve the earth would make a big jerk and turn the other way to begin a new year. Of course I never had a chance to actually experience the movement, because I was usually sound asleep by then. Later, when I was allowed to stay up to have a toast with my parents and Renee, sipping pink Champagne, and when the man on the radio announced the New Year at midnight, I realized that there was no jerk or any kind of a movement. The world didn't shift after all!

However, even without that, those nights were always exciting experiences, for after midnight,

Dad would have us each melt a piece of lead on a spoon over the hot stove. The molten metal was dumped into a bowl of ice water. The lead would then form strange effigies and it was left to our imagination to figure out what the newly formed lead resembled – to determine what the next year had in store for each of us. If the shape resembled a boat, for example, a cruise might be indicated. A car or train could mean a move of some sort, and so on. This *Bleigiessen* was a fun entertainment that was actually taken halfway seriously.

What was the coming year going to bring for us here in the camp? Were we going to be free? Was this misery going to come to an end?

"Let's keep up our good spirits," Mutti urged, wiping our and her own tears. "God will guide us through this, as he has done so far. We have conquered all the hardship until now and we will see it through till it's over. As long as we have faith, and have each other, all will be well in the end!"

Mother didn't make speeches like that very often. That was quite a resolution she made for us. And strength and hope derived from her words for me as we hugged and kissed under tears when the Master of Ceremony announced the New Year 1946.

Chapter Sixteen

"I Can Do With You As I Please, You German Pig!"

Shortly after New Year's, Renee and I were put into "permanent" jobs.

It was a tearful goodbye from Mother. We hated to leave her alone in her frail condition, and we hoped that we would be able to come back occasionally to be with her. However, that was questionable because both our assignments were about twenty miles away and the permissions to use the train were very limited.

With the shiny white ribbon on my arm, I boarded the railroad car accompanied by the farmer's young son who had come to get me. He was a silent, brooding person and didn't speak one word to me on the whole trip.

'Oh dear,' I thought to myself. 'If this is an indication of what the next few weeks are going to be like, I don't seem to be able to look forward to a very pleasant time.'

From the station in the village we had to walk about five miles to his farm. The snow on the unplowed road made walking very difficult. A blustery wind found its way through my coat to my skinny body and forced tears into my eyes. The young man, Janush, tried to beat the wind by walking extremely fast and I could barely keep up with him.

"Please, don't go so fast, I can't keep up with you," I pleaded.

"I want to get home," he replied. "I am cold!" (He actually had a voice and could speak!) "You better lift your lazy bones, and move!"

When we finally arrived at the farm, a huge turkey greeted us in the barnyard, flapping his wings and stretching his neck angrily. Until then I had never seen a live turkey and this hostile fellow really scared me. I felt like turning around and running, and in the following nine weeks that I spent there, Mr. Gobble-Gobble and I never became friends.

The farmer's lady was a chubby person with a very round face and a handkerchief on her head at all times. I never saw her without it and I suspected she even slept with it.

"*Dobry rano,*" Good morning, she greeted me. "I will show you where you are going to sleep."

I was lodged in a storage room, adjacent to

the hallway. Next to the potatoes, onions and cabbages, was a huge bed with an enormous feather comforter. It smelled musty in there, and the room had no stove or heater.

"You will wash up in the barn," she said when I looked for a washbasin or sink. Then she added: "You will be a great help for us, I hope."

Her husband had had a stroke recently and walked with a cane. He was quite bitter about his condition and let everybody know by being bossy and ornery.

Having grown up in the city, I had never gotten near any farm animals. Cows as well as pigs and turkeys I knew only from pictures, or at best had seen them in the countryside while riding a train.

Now I was put in charge of fourteen oversized, dumb-looking, mooing, chewing, plump monsters, lined up against the wall in a dark smelly barn! The young farmer showed me how to use a pitchfork to get the smelly gook away from under the cow's hoofs, and I could tell that he was very disgusted about my stupidity not to know how to do that in the first place.

The trough was built against the wall, so the cows had to be shoved over from one side to the other in order to dump the baskets of hay and feed in front of their ever-chewing mouths. The water pails had to go in the same way, and more often than once, a shower of cold water ended up all over me instead of in the trough when one of the cows decided to push back at me. A small hand pump by the door was to be my bath and the outhouse was located in one corner of the barnyard next to the manure pit.

The first days went fairly well. I tried as well as I could to learn what I was expected to do, even though deep down I thoroughly resented the whole thing. Why in the world should I have to clean out this filthy cow-barn, and scrub the rough kitchen floor while the lady of the house sat on top of the huge bake oven, praying her rosary all day!

There were times when I figured she had to do this, to pray for forgiveness for treating me so poorly. She was a poor cook besides, and even though I was allowed to eat with them at the table in the beginning, after a short while they decided I should eat my meals in the hall. It was cold out there and the portions became smaller and smaller. To keep the hunger down as much as possible, I started stealing food. When the woman gave me a large piece of bread to give to the dog, the poor critter got only half it.

"I am sorry, Puppy, I have to keep myself alive somehow," I would explain, and eat the other half.

The potatoes and onions in my room helped a little, even though I hated onions, and raw potatoes are no delicacy at all. I even learned to eat raw eggs, and when I went to gather them, one or two always ended up in my stomach.

One morning, while I was cleaning the barn, the cow at the very end of the line got mad at me for some reason and instead of moving over so I could work around her, she moved closer to me and squeezed me against the wall. Her hind part on my chest pinned me against the cold stones at my back. The pitchfork had fallen to the floor and my only defense was my hands. Clenching them into fists, I pounded on that clumsy piece of beef with all the strength I could muster, and underlined my action with loud screams. Janush came and got me out of my predicament none too soon.

"Don't you know you have to be careful with that bull?" he yelled.

Well, that of course was news to me. To me the animals all looked alike, and even though I was aware that a male cow was a bull, and was sensitive to the color red, I couldn't tell which was which! Until then I had no idea that I had taken care of the boss of the barn the whole time.

The situation didn't improve and the worst thing was that I had no connection whatsoever with my mother or my sister. I tried to write some letters, but they never got out, mainly because I had no money for the postage and the farmer was not about to finance anything for me.

One morning, when I carried the heavy milk can to the delivery point by the road, I met a neighbor. We started talking and it turned out that she was not at all fond of my employer.

"He is a despicable old cuss," she stated. "And you sure got yourself a nasty job there."

I had written a letter to Mother and on one of the following mornings I worked up enough courage and handed it to the woman.

"Will you please put this in the mail for me? I

pleaded. And then I added, "I have no money, though."

Her reaction surprised me.

"Huh!" she exclaimed. "I will take care of that for sure! I'd do anything to get back at this old goat." She was referring to my farmer, but did not explain what caused her hostility. But it didn't matter to me, as long as my message got to the camp.

I didn't hear anything for a long time. Finally, one morning my new friend waved an envelop at me.

"I hope it is good news," she said.

Oh, it sure was!

Renee had written this letter on one of her visits to see Mother. She had been much luckier than I in regard to her assignment. Her job was at a mill and all she had to do was take care of a baby. She was treated very well, got plenty to eat, and the miller even gave her some pocket money. In addition to that, he took her occasionally to the camp to see Mother. When I opened the page, a 5.00 Korona bill fell out. "Maybe you can put the money to good use somehow, and I hope it will help you in your desperate position," she wrote.

I cried and kissed the letter and pressed it against my chest. "You dear, dear sister," I whispered. I had to keep the money well hidden and was not sure what I was going to do with it at the time but I knew it was going to come in handy someday.

Then I read on and more good news revealed itself.

Mother had recovered a little and was able to work again. They had put her back into the kitchen, which of course had a very good effect on her. Not only did she get better and more food, but it also helped her emotionally.

The letter was a real treasure and in the following weeks I read it over and over again, as the circumstances worsened more and more.

At the end of February, we were threshing one afternoon. Snow was still on the ground and it was very cold. The wooden-soled shoes I had when I first came there had lost their bottoms and the farmer's lady had given me a pair of old felt boots in a spurt of generosity. But they had holes all the way around, so the water and the snow found their way to my freezing toes.

The air was clear but the dust from the threshing darkened the sky. Four nasty turkeys scratched the ground in the meadow and became annoying with their constant gobble-gobble. I tried to chase them, or at least quiet them by throwing snowballs at them. But that only caused them to increase the volume of their infernal noise. I would have liked to wring their skinny necks!

However, I didn't have much time to worry about the turkeys, for work was to be done and the old farmer made sure that it was not neglected. With his cane, he directed the whole operation and the words he used to drive us on were not exactly choice.

Somehow, a piece of straw, like a splinter, got into the forefinger of my left hand. It hurt a little and I pulled it out. But apparently I didn't get the whole thing because the next day my finger was badly infected. When I showed it to the farmer he only laughed.

"Sissy city kid," he said. "Piss on it, it'll go away."

I asked for hot water and soap to soak it, but no—.

"You wash where you always wash, and where you belong – in the barn!" was the answer.

My hands and feet had gotten very rough and were black from washing with cold water all the time. I was never able to get the dirt completely off my skin. The corners on my fingernails had gotten sore, and on the bottoms of my feet the skin had cracked all around big calluses.

The pain in my infected finger got worse every day and at night the throbbing would keep me awake.

"I will take you to the doctor," the farmer said one morning.

For a moment hope came up for me on the horizon. My heart jumped for joy. I would go back to the camp, see my mother and sister again, and maybe, just maybe would not have to go back to this place! But I rejoiced too early. It seemed he had the same idea as I and didn't want to take the chance of losing me.

"Oh no," he laughed, "not the camp doctor. We see our country doctor in the village, or nothing doing!"

I chose the latter and my finger kept on throbbing.

Time went on and it was now over two months that I had been working there. It was the beginning of March, the snow started melting and only occasional flurries of snow mixed with rain indicated that winter was not quite over yet.

Mardi Gras was going on and the young farmer went every night into the village to celebrate.

One afternoon I was chopping wood by the shed when the old man came to join me. If it was to check on me, keep me company or just pick on me, I didn't know. We got to talking.

"You know, you are pretty well off here," he boasted. "The people in Germany are very poor and don't have anything to eat.

"Well, I am not exactly overfed here," I argued. "And anyway, at least they are free out there!"

The slavery-like conditions that went on ever since we were arrested and the fact that my hand was in a stage of painful soreness, made me angry and brave. We were in the tenth month of imprisonment and it seemed so unjust and senseless to keep us like that without any trial or explanation.

"I would rather by hungry out there than have to serve you here with just as little to eat!" I don't know where I got the courage to say this, but in my anger and desperation I felt my temper swelling. I wanted to say more but the farmer interrupted me. Stepping close to me he started swinging his cane.

"How dare you talk to me like that," he yelled. "You German pig, I can do with you as I please," and only because my feet were faster than his was he prevented from really hitting me.

I ran across the barnyard. The only place I felt safe from his threat was the outhouse. It was the only place I could lock behind me. I stayed there for a while, until I thought that the old man might have cooled down. But when I came out and stepped into the house, he started yelling and raving again.

"No supper for you tonight!" he shouted and waving his cane, he started out after me again.

"Finish your chores, you German sow! And stay out of my sight!"

Now tears of anger swelled up in my eyes. To be called a pig had gotten rather routine, but now I had advanced to a sow!

I clenched my fists and ran into the barn. In my desperation I hugged one of the young heifers. Her neck felt smooth and warm and the whole misery of my situation came clear to me again. There I was hugging a lowly cow, crying bitter tears on her neck!

"I just can't stand this any more," I sobbed into her ear. "I can't stay here any longer!"

And right then I decided that the time had come to leave this inhospitable place. I had to find a way to get back to the camp!

CHAPTER SEVENTEEN

THE ESCAPE.

It was the third of March, Maundy Tuesday, the last day of Mardi Gras. It didn't really make any difference what day it was. I had made up my mind that this was the time to use my 5.00 Koronas. After what happened in the woodshed that afternoon, I decided this was the night to run away.

With my clothes on, I lay down on my bed to wait for the proper time when everything would be quiet in the house. I was worried that I might fall asleep, but the excitement kept me alert. Also, the palm of my hand had gotten very tender and slightly red, and the throbbing had moved into my arm.

It was after midnight when I finally felt safe enough to sneak out the back door. There was still light shining through the kitchen window. Janush had gone to a party again and apparently his mother was waiting up for him – most likely sitting on top of the bake oven, praying her rosary.

The dog gave a soft growl when I opened the gate, but calmed down when he recognized me.

It was a dark, windy night. Light snow fell mixed with rain. The slush on the ground made walking very unpleasant. My feet got wet and soon my whole body was cold and uncomfortable. But if I wanted to follow through with my plan I had to keep going.

I had walked for about two miles when I saw in the distance a person coming down the road toward me.

'This might be Janush coming home from his party,' I thought.

I could only hope that I had seen him before he was aware of me. My heart was way up in my throat as I went quickly down the embankment, hiding behind some bushes, sinking knee-deep into the snow bank. I didn't dare breathe and my heart beat so loudly that I was afraid it would give me away. The person came closer and closer. It was a man, and by his singing and the way he was walking, I concluded that indeed he had been to a party. As he passed barely three feet from my hideout I recognized Janush. He didn't see me, but just to make sure, I waited until I could not see him anymore before I went back out onto the road.

My slacks and the heavy underwear had soaked up the water from the snow and I was drenched all the way up to my hips.

The wind picked up and my feet started to hurt. A chill went into my bones and stayed there. All of a sudden a piercing pain went into my hand and up into my arm.

"Dear Lord, please help me! I've got to get to that train station – it can't be much further!" Tears started running down my face and I felt very weak.

"Please help me, Lord!" I kept repeating. I couldn't think of another prayer. My legs felt like heavy lead weights and sudden chills made me shiver until my teeth chattered.

Finally, I saw lights in the distance. I felt a little better, just knowing that I soon would be at the first stop of my adventure. When I reached the village, the church clock struck three o'clock. It was much too early for the first train.

The depot was dark and no conductor or clerk was anywhere in sight. The schedule on the wall indicated that the next rain to Bistrice was to leave at five-thirty.

That was two and a half hours away! What was I going to do all that time in this dark depot, wet and hungry?

Hungry!

By God, all of a sudden I realized how hungry I was. The fact that I didn't have supper that night became a painful reminder of my stomach.

I felt sick and had to sit down on one of the benches in the waiting area. A dizzy feeling started to spin in my head. You must not faint, not now, certainly not here!

I tried to imagine seeing my mother again, and green grass and blooming flowers, and sunshine, and hearing birds sing. It took a few attempts until I finally managed to get to my feet. I was still somewhat dizzy and now my feet were numb, and it felt like I was walking on cotton.

I stepped out onto the sidewalk. On the other side of the street was the bright light of a small pub. The loud music as well as the loud voices indicated that for some people Mardi Gras was not over yet. Half in a daze, I walked across and stepped into the pub. There was a happy bunch of people, dancing, drinking and singing. The room was full of smoke and the air smelled of wine and liquor.

I sat down at a table nearby and a chubby, friendly-looking man with a big apron stepped up to me and asked me for my order.

"I would like a sandwich and a glass of milk, please."

A big smile came to his face as he hurried off to get what I had asked for. I guess it must have seemed funny to him to want a glass of milk at a time like this in the middle of all these more or less drunken guests. It wasn't very long when he came back with my sandwich and, placing it and the milk in front of me, he sat down himself sizing me curiously, obviously trying hard to control his desire to ask some questions.

I didn't care at the moment. I was sick from hunger. My hand gave me considerable pain and the chills started running up and down my back again. In short, I felt miserable! But a big gulp of milk put some life back into me and the sandwich tasted like manna from heaven.

I must have really made some impression on the man. As soon as I had finished, he got up without a word and came back after a short while with another sandwich and steaming bowl of soup. The whole time he kept staring at my hands until he couldn't hold his curiosity back anymore.

"You sure have rough hands," he said. "It looks like you did pretty hard work lately."

"Yes," I answered between bites. "I worked on a farm."

I couldn't tell him where I came from or where I was going, and all of a sudden his presence made me very uneasy.

"So where are you headed?"

There it was! The question I had feared. What was I going to say? For a moment I drew a blank. Think Elga, think! What shall I tell him? If I told the truth he would call the constable for sure! Think Elga, think!

There were two camps in the area at that time. The one in Bistrice where I was based, and one about twenty miles farther north in Beneshov, where Austrian citizens were held. News had come that the camp in Beneshov was to be dissolved and the prisoners released and sent back to Austria. Like a flash, that came to my mind. I boldly lied:

"I am Austrian and I am coming back from my farm assignment. Our camp in Beneshov is being dissolved."

If he believed this story or if he just was a

nice man, I don't know. His only comment to my explanation was: "Oh, I see." But he didn't sound very convinced.

I paid my bill and then I saw the innkeeper talking to another man and pointing at me.

Suddenly I realized how foolish I had been, jeopardizing my escape by walking into what had to turn out to be a trap. Terror struck me again and I couldn't get out of there fast enough.

"Please Lord, don't let them catch me!"

Pictures of torture and beatings of runaways popped into my mind. The refreshing feeling I had gotten after I ate gave way to a paralyzing fear.

'They can't catch me now, I am almost there!'

As calmly as I could, I walked out of the pub and went to the depot to purchase my ticket.

Don't panic, just don't panic!

I had no idea what it would cost, and I hadn't planned on buying two sandwiches. As I crossed the street I heard footsteps behind me.

"I hear you are going to Beneshov," a young voice asked. "Would you like some company?"

Now, if t here was anything I did not need at this point, it was company. The young man seemed friendly enough, but on the other hand I wasn't in the habit of seeking young men's company at four o'clock in the morning.

"No, thank you." I made my point clear to that effect.

"You really shouldn't be traveling alone at this time of the night," he insisted. After a second refusal, he left me alone. However, he didn't go back to the inn but stood behind me at the ticket counter.

"One way to Beneshov, please," I requested, knowing that he was watching, and I had just enough money left.

"You are really going to Beneshov," he said with astonishment in his voice as I stepped away from the counter.

"That's what I told the Innkeeper, didn't I?" was my reply. "Didn't he believe me?" And then I added daringly: "Why are you spying on me?"

I figured offense might be the best defense in this situation, and I was right. The young man blushed, apologized, and to my surprise and great relief, retreated back to the pub.

But I still had an hour to wait and chances of being discovered increased the longer I was in one spot. I thought of the farmer and I hoped that he wouldn't become aware of my escape until daylight. And that he would not catch up with me until I was back in the safety of the camp.

It was an awfully long hour as I sat there in the dark corner, tired and wet, shivering from the cold. I feared also that somebody might get suspicious and call the constable.

In the excitement, I had forgotten about my hand. But sitting there in the cold waiting room I could feel it all the way up in my shoulder. The lymph nodes in my armpit started to hurt, too. What if I had blood poisoning and would lose my arm? I could even die if I didn't get help soon!

At some point in the past months death had seemed like an easy solution to our problems, but at the moment I was not too keen about the idea. I had gotten that far after the bad experience of the nine weeks on the farm, had walked the five grueling miles through he cold, wet night. I couldn't bear the thought of giving up now.

I got up from the hard bench and started walking up and down. I was very warm all of a sudden, and the notes and posters on the walls reached enormous proportions, and seemed to be moving closer and closer. I stepped outside for some fresh air. It was still very dark except for the dim lantern that illuminated the railroad platform. A light drizzle fell through the morning mist. There was nobody around. The train wasn't due for another half hour.

The young man who was so eager to keep me company had gone back to the inn. The ticket office attendant had closed his window and I could see him sleeping on a cot in the back room.

After a while I heard the train whistle in the distance. Was this night really going to end? Would I finally be able to get on the train and in a few hours hug my mother and sister again? Would my luck hold out for a little while longer, or would I encounter some more close calls?

There was the whistle again, this time much closer, and soon the locomotive came into view. Huffing and puffing, it pulled only a few passenger cars and about six freight cars. Another chill hit me again, my hands trembled, and I almost missed the handrail that led into the compartment. I was in a complete daze when I finally sat down on a seat near the window. I had to make sure not to miss my destination. My head hurt. I was tired. And I could feel that I was running a temperature.

I must have dozed off for a while, for when I opened my eyes, it was daylight. The train had stopped and looking out I could see that we were in a small station.

'Oh God, where am I? Did I miss getting off?'

The sign under the roof read "Bistrice."

Bistrice! I had to get out!

I jumped up too fast and a dizzy spell sent me back in my seat. On the second try, I got to my feet and scrambled out through the narrow hallway. People had already boarded the train and were in my way. I collided with a number of them. I heard the conductor blow the whistle for the engineer to move on, and the locomotive started to roll just as I reached the platform.

The drizzle had stopped, but it was slippery. Jumping off the moving train, I fell as I reached the ground. People gathered around me to see if I was all right and the stationmaster gave me an unfriendly *Sacramenska holka* greeting. Darned girl. I certainly didn't need all that attention. The less people knew about me, the better chances I had to get away with my escapade.

Not too much could happen to me anymore since I was so close to the camp. But then, in a brief flash, the "Bunker" came to mind, the cell in the camp where runaways had to suffer bitter consequences. I tried to tell myself that I didn't really run away, I was turning myself in. There should be a difference! But then I wasn't sure.

All of a sudden a cold fear grabbed my heart: what if they send me back to the farmer? Will they torture and beat me as they did all the others who had tried to run away. But then again, I didn't run away from the camp! Oh, if I only knew!

Somebody helped me up. My left knee was bruised and my head still hurt. The station house and all the people around me were in a haze. I could hardly see them. My legs gave in and I fell back to the ground.

"Ta holka je nemocna," somebody said. This girl is sick. "Somebody should call a doctor."

With all the strength I could muster, I forced myself up.

"Oh no, I am all right," I declared. "And thank you. *Djekuji.*"

Then I started walking. Or did I stagger? My feet were as heavy as lead and each step caused me pain all through my body.

The sun had risen and promised a new day. Like so many times in the past year, the sun somehow encouraged me. It was always the symbol of a new beginning. And in spite of my ill feeling, hope came back to my heart.

"I will face whatever will happen!" I whispered bravely to myself. My legs were still heavy, but my vision had improved. I could see where I was going.

When I finally arrived at the camp gate a number of inmates came out on their way to their assignments.

"Oh, will your mother be glad to see you!" one of them exclaimed when she saw me.

"How come, you are without a guard or your farmer?" another one wanted to know. But before I could tell them what I had done, the guard drove them on to go ahead.

I passed through the gate. It was like reaching the goal in a foot race, and after I had walked a few steps I collapsed and everything became black around me.

I woke up from something warm dripping on my face. Mother was bent over me, calling my name, her voice choked by tears.

"Oh Mutti, will they send me back? Please, don't let them send me back!"

"Everything will be all right," she assured me. "Just relax. They are going to operate on your finger. You seem to have blood poisoning."

I looked around. I was in the infirmary and my friend Inge put something on my face. It got dark around me again and faintly I heard her say: "Please, count backwards from 99."

"99, 98, 97" I started, half in a daze already. I don't know how far I got before the anesthetic took effect.

CHAPTER EIGHTEEN

BITTERSWEET.

The surgery of my finger had gone fairly well. They had to remove the nail and seemed to have done a good job.

I was surprised about the changes; not only of attitude, but also in the way the inmates were treated. I had been away from the camp for over two months. In the meantime, the commandant had been replaced at the intervention of representatives of the International Red Cross, which had held several inspection tours and strongly objected to conditions.

The new commandant apparently had more humane points of view. Generally, the food supply was better and the overall treatment wasn't as cruel and severe as it had been before.

All my fears about possible reprisals were unfounded, for nobody even gave it a thought to punish me. As a matter of fact, everybody treated me with great concern and tenderness. I was allowed to stay in the infirmary for a whole week, got double rations of food, and when the farmer came back after me, he was told that he wasn't going to be able to get another worker ever again.

My recovery went well, and after I moved back to the barracks to live with Mother, I was fairly free to move around in the camp.

One beautiful morning, I strolled down to the south end. The snow was gone and the ice on the lake had melted. The water was sparkling and glistened from the glow of the morning light. A lark sang his praises above in the cloudless blue sky. A patch of little flowers had boldly formed a yellow circle in the wet grass. It reminded me of the Easter mornings when our father used to take us for our traditional Easter egg hunts.

We would board the street car and go to the end of the line where there were no more houses, just white birch trees with little yellow seeds hanging from their branches. In the meadow was a little creek and cheerful birds were singing jubilantly in the trees.

"Let's walk into the meadow," Dad would suggest, and we would walk a little distance. And even though the ground was still wet and muddy, and white patches of melting snow were scattered between thin blades of tender grass, small bunches of violets and snowdrops surprised our searching eyes and promised new life after a long, cold winter. A perfect place to find the Easter Bunny.

We all started searching. We searched on the ground, in the bushes, up in the tree branches, and Dad seemed to be putting more effort into it than either one of us children. Oddly enough though, he didn't find a single egg, or chocolate bunny, or grass nest with Easter eggs. However, his large coat pockets would get strangely flat after a while. When our baskets were filled, we would sit down on a fallen tree and would start tasting our goodies. Then we would head for the streetcar and go home again.

As I walked through the camp, that ground was still wet and muddy, too. The grass had started to turn green, and spring flowers appeared in small numbers. It was the end of March – Easter could not be far away. Holidays didn't have much meaning anymore since any kind of religious services, even on Sundays, were forbidden to us, and the little church in the village had closed its doors to the camp inmates. It was easy to lose track of time.

But nature obviously celebrated the beginning of spring, creation of new life, the rising of the Lord, and the promise of hope.

Hope? – Hope for what? An end of this misery we had been living for the last eleven months?

Was the end of this winter going to bring an end to our imprisonment? All we had left was hope, and as I hiked through the wet grass I prayed: Lord, don't let me despair, but bring us the freedom that you are demonstrating in the awakening of nature all around me.

I came to a deserted area, just grass and a few bushes. In the corner, right next to the barbed wire fence, was a lonely building, a shelter house with three open walls. It had no floor, and the ground was as wet and muddy as on the outside. On the only wall were shelves, wide enough to hold a human body.

Usually we tried to avoid going there. The place was taboo, and the guards could become very indignant when they found anybody in its vicinity. Secretly, it was called "The Chamber of Death," for it was the place where the sick were taken when there was no more hope for recovery. They were just put there, and left to die.

I stepped inside. A strange power seemed to draw me nearer to the wall. Three bodies were lying on the shelf – motionless. Terror struck me and I wanted to turn around and run away, back outside where there was life, and hope, and sunshine, and singing birds!

A weak moan came from one of the bodies. I turned and stepped closer, feeling very uneasy and scared.

It was an old woman, at least she seemed very old to me. Dirty rags were wrapped around her. Her face was ashen gray, her cheeks were fallen in deeply, and her eyes were so far back in her head that I could hardly see them. Two flies were buzzing over her face and her straggly, filthy hair was infested with lice.

I made another step toward her, and there I saw a number of fleas sitting on her neck. I wanted to turn around, but she was still alive, and I leaned over close enough so she could see me. Weakly she raised her hand and grabbed mine. It was ice cold, and her grip made me shiver.

"Water," I could hear her whisper, and it seemed like her dying eyes had a light shining in them. Now I realized that she had my hand in an iron hold. Her strength was unbelievable. It seemed unreal.

"Let me go!" I yelled in terror. "I will get you some water!"

Her mouth moved again, without a sound. Then her head fell to the side, and her eyes turned dead. I had seen death repeatedly since we had been imprisoned, but all I felt at this moment was relief, and thankfulness that her sufferings were over.

I sank to my knees, her bony fingers still clutching my hand.

"Dear father in heaven...." I started.

A harsh voice interrupted me: "What in the world are you doing here? Don't you know you are not allowed here? Get out before I used this on you!" He swung his whip, and before I could duck, he hit me hard on my back.

I got up and tried to loosen the dead woman's clasp; for all that time she had held onto me. The guard stood in awe. He didn't know what to say when he saw that I had to pry one finger at a time from my hand.

"Was she a relative of yours?" he inquired,

and for a moment his voice was almost human.

"She was a sister – a sister in suffering."

Then I walked out of the shelter house, back into the sunny, beautiful day.

The whole episode must have taken only a few minutes, a few minutes that seemed like a lifetime – that ended a lifetime. A nightmare that was real, as real as the sun, the lark, the little yellow flowers, the spring, and the beginning of new life.

And our lives went on.

Those prisoners who had survived eleven months of hardship tried to hold on a little longer. About half of the inmates were gone. Most of them had died; some had been released. There were many empty bunks in the barracks.

Renee and I didn't know how long Mother would be able to last. She had gotten thinner and thinner. However, she seemed to have come to peace with the fact that Dad was gone. She had realized that she had us to live for, and had given up her gloomy thoughts about killing herself.

But Mother's body seemed to wither away more and more every day. She was too weak to do any kind of work, and even her job in the kitchen became too much for her.

Renee, who still had her "steady" work assignment in the mill, was allowed to visit us every Sunday. These were exciting highlights, and since she could bring all kinds of food, these weekends could easily be considered lifesavers for Mother.

CHAPTER NINETEEN

WILL TOMORROW BE BETTER, AFTER ALL?

Soon after, I was informed that I was lazy long enough.

My finger had healed, leaving an ugly scar, but other than being hungry all the time and grossly undernourished, there was nothing physically wrong with me. I had lost a lot of weight, but I had always been skinny and was never very strong.

I hated to leave mother alone in her weak condition and for a moment I hated myself for not giving in to one of the leading "trusties." I could really be having a good life with all I wanted to eat for myself and for Mother, and wouldn't even have to work for it. All I would have to do was follow one of them into his bunk.

These kinds of liaisons happened all over the camp, and deep down in my heart I wished I could do it, too. There was a difference between the rapes by the Russians and a relationship, or even a one-night-stand within the camp; it happened very seldom that these men forced themselves on a girl that wasn't willing to go along. They didn't have to. There were plenty that saw the advantages, and justified their actions with the circumstances.

But to me love, real love, had to come first and never was I going to have sex willingly to satisfy mine or someone else's physical needs. And even though life was much easier for those who consented, it just didn't seem right to me to do something that was against everything that my parents had taught me about human value.

On the other hand, some of the affairs became quite serious and ended in lifetime commitments after we were released and ministers became available to join them officially as husband and wife.

I had formed a warm friendship with Bruno. His material contributions had helped me repeatedly, and his quiet way of understanding was of great comfort to me. Often he held me in his arms, and it felt secure and pleasant. However, he never made any sexual advances, and that made him even more dear.

I went to look for him, to ask him to keep an eye on Mother while I was gone, but found out that he, too, was assigned to a "permanent" job.

A guard came and urged me to follow him. With an emotional embrace, tears quelling in my eyes, I kissed Mother goodbye.

"Take care, Mutti, I hope I will be back soon."

"God be with you!" she sobbed, and pressed me to her chest as if she never would let me go.

"All right, enough of this!" the guard exclaimed, and grabbed me by the shoulder.

The man who had "rented" me to be a housemaid for his family was waiting impatiently in the office. We walked to the station and boarded the train. The ribbon on my left arm was white and shiny. The people looked at me in disgust and contempt. I don't know why they were not used to us German prisoners by now. After all, we had been a familiar sight in their neighborhood for almost a year, and none of us had asked to be there! I'd leave right now if they wanted to get rid of me! Oh, how I wished that I could spit in their faces! However, I had learned the hard way to control my feelings, so all these revolting thoughts were only in my mind while I stood shy and humbly in the train corridor.

The ride took only fifteen minutes. Mr. Svoboda's grocery store was located on the main street in the village. His wife was young and pretty, and their three-year-old daughter was hiding halfway behind her mother, holding onto her apron, giving me a shy, inquisitive look.

Mr. Svoboda's mother lived with them and she was the only person who couldn't get herself to be friendly with me as long as I stayed there. The rest of them, even the neighbors, became rather nice after only a few days. For the first time I could eat as much as I wanted and nobody called me a "pig" or swung a whip or cane at me. I had to do all the housework, wash and iron, and even though the house was small, it was hard and strenuous work for me. Every night I fell exhausted into the clean bed in the tiny room next to the kitchen.

Obviously, I hadn't regained all my strength after my bout with blood poisoning and the operation. My undernourished condition could not provide any stamina. But at least I was treated decently and had enough to eat. I no longer had to steal onions or raw potatoes and raw eggs to keep me going.

The good life lasted three weeks. Then one morning Mr. Svoboda came with great tidings.

"The camp in Bistrice is going to be dissolved and you are going to be released," he said. "I will take you back this afternoon. Try to get your chores done, so we can leave right after lunch."

The frequent inspections of the camp by members of the International Red Cross in the past certainly had been clear indications that something was being done toward our release, and for months I had been waiting for this news. But now I didn't believe it.

"Ya, sure," was all I could say, contemplating what other possible reason could there be for calling me back. Maybe Mother was very ill. Could she have died? However, normally the administration did not bother to inform the absent family of the passing of a member. Even though conditions in the camp had improved considerably in the past two months, that practice had not changed.

I wish you could stay with us a little longer," Mr. Svoboda stated while I did the dishes after lunch. "My little Marisha got to like you very much!"

On the other hand, the older Mrs. Svoboda gave the little bundle of my belongings a thorough check-up, and when she found nothing that didn't belong to me she concluded with an approving nod of her head: "I guess you are not a thief after all."

'Well, I am sure glad I convinced you of that,' I thought to myself, resenting her humoring me. And for her sake I was happy that my time there was finished.

Mr. Svoboda and I left, and when we arrived at the camp after the short train ride I could see that something was going on. I was not the only one to be called back in the middle of the week.

We checked in at the office.

I said goodbye to Mr. Svoboda, and he left. A number of other inmates were standing there, and with a little speech, the commandant explained to us that, indeed, the camp was closing and we were on our way to Germany. He looked friendly and sounded quite sincere, so I decided to believe him. All the other people around me broke out in shouts of joy.

On the way to the barracks, I stumbled and fell to the ground. My feet could not run as fast as I wanted them to and I couldn't be soon enough in my mother's arms.

"Mutti," I called out as I approached the building.

"Mutti!"

But there was no response. She must be somewhere around in the camp, I thought, and stepped into the open door.

There, a strange feeling came over me. I sensed a disturbing difference. I could not pinpoint it, but something just didn't feel right. There were only a few women in their bunks, and when I came to the bunk Mother had occupied, it was empty. The blanket and all her belongings were gone.

"Did my mother move somewhere else?" I asked the woman in the next bunk. She had tears in her eyes. Panic grabbed my heart.

"Frau Schenk, where is my mother?"

And when she didn't answer right away, I screamed at her: "Where is my mother? Did my sister come back from her job? And where is she?"

Frau Schenk's voice was choked with tears when she finally answered: "They both had to leave yesterday on the first transport. Your mother tried to explain that you should come with them, but nobody listened to her and she and your sister had to go."

For a moment I thought the earth was going to open up and I would sink into a deep hole. The room around me started to twirl in a circle and there was a strange feeling in my stomach. My head felt like it was going to burst.

Very faintly I heard Frau Schenk's voice.

"Your mother left you a note," she said, and handed me a piece of paper. Tears filled my eyes when I saw Mother's handwriting. I couldn't read it, and handed the note back to the woman. She started reading: "My dear little one," but my sobbing made her stop.

All of a sudden, a wave of anger went through me, much like the time when I last saw my father in the prison in Prague. How could they do this to us? Who do they think they are, manipulating our lives like this! Haven't we suffered enough? First they killed Dad, and now they think they can tear us apart!

In the past months I had learned to control my temper – the hard way – but this was just too much to bear!

I stormed out of the door to the administration office. The guard at the door stopped me. In my desperation, I reached for his rifle.

"I have to see the commandant, my family is gone!" I screamed. "I want to know how this could happen! Let me in, I have to talk to him!"

Probably wondering about the commotion, the commandant stepped out of his office.

"My family is gone!" I yelled again. "How could you do this to me?"

Now, this behavior was open rebellion in the eyes of the office. After all, I was still a prisoner! He looked at me coldly.

"Take her to the bunker," was all he said. And while I was kicking and screaming, the guard dragged me to a cold cell.

Now what?

I sat there on the cot for a while, crying

bitterly until there were no more tears. Slowly I calmed down and there I noticed that I still had Mother's note crumbled up in my fist.

"My dear little one," I started again. "This can only be a short note, for as usual, everything has to go fast – except waiting of course. Renee and I were chosen to go on the first transport without you. I could not convince them to let us wait. Believe me, I tried! They say that they are taking us to Prague to a camp where they gather people from all other camps, to ship us all together to Germany. Let's try and find each other there. God willing, we will! Hold on, and try to be patient, my darling. Our thoughts are with you. Mother."

And there was a line from Renee: "Mutti is very desperate, but she believes we will be together again. Have courage, and try not to lose your temper. Renee."

How well she knew me, and how confident she sounded. How can we possibly find each other in a camp with thousands of people!

"If you believe in something strongly enough, it will come true," was another one of father's mottos. God knows, I had wished strongly for us to be together with him again, but it wouldn't be in this world. And that's what counts right now! This world and all the mean people in it, and all the ugly things that keep happening to us! Mother's note gave me only a little confidence. I was discouraged and bitter.

I lay awake on the cot for most of the night, and it was dusk *(dawn?)* when I finally dozed off. In my sleep, I dreamed I was chasing a freight train that went faster and faster and no matter how hard I tried, I could not catch up with it. My legs were as heavy as millstones, and eventually the train disappeared on the horizon. It was hopeless to follow anymore, so I gave up and sat down on the tracks, completely out of breath, my heart heavy, tears running down my cheeks.

All of a sudden, Dad stood next to me. I felt his hand on my shoulder and looked up into his face. He looked as drawn and unshaven as I had seen him in Prague, and his eyes were very sad. His lips formed a faint smile that seemed to move further and further away. Then he shook my shoulder and called out to me.

"Wake up, wake up!"

As I opened my eyes, the guard stood bent over me.

"You can go to the barracks now, if you promise to behave," he said. "The next transport leaves tomorrow and you will be on it."

I knew Dad was with me, so I gathered some courage and asked, "Could I speak to the commandant?"

"I doubt that he will speak to you after your outburst yesterday," the man replied, but looking at my tear-covered face, he must have seen the desperation in my eyes.

"All right, I will ask him," he consented.

He left, leaving the cell door open, and I stepped out into the hallway. I was trembling in anticipation. What was I going to say to the man?

Why did I even ask to have an audience? The guard came back and said: "You have five minutes."

With weak knees and my heart beating all the way up into my throat again, I walked into his office. His, "So, what do you want now?" was not at all encouraging.

"Please," I started, my voice but a whisper. All my bravery seemed to have left me, my anger had turned into desperation, and all I could feel was my loneliness and being completely helpless.

"*Prosim*," I whispered again in his language. "How will I find my mother? Please, help me!" Asking this man for help was just like asking for the moon, and I knew that, but it was the only thing I could think of. He looked at me in astonishment. He probably thought I was out of my mind.

"How am I supposed to do that?" he asked with a smirk on his face.

I had a good notion to tell him if he hadn't sent Mother and Renee away in the first place, we wouldn't have this problem. But under the circumstances, I decided to be quiet. It was definitely better to use a little diplomacy now instead of outbursts of anger.

"Where were they taken?" I asked. "Surely you know that, you are the commandant." The expression on his face showed me that I had indeed struck the right note.

"Well," he answered, "of course I know that. There is a collecting camp in Prague where all the Germans are taken. That's where you will go tomorrow with the rest of the people. Maybe you will find your family there."

'Does this man realize how slim my chances are?' I thought to myself. 'Big help he is!'

"But how?" was my next question. "How can I find them among thousands of people?"

His next answer was much friendlier.

"Well," he said again. "This whole thing is organized by the International Red Cross, and I am sure they have all the people registered. So when you get there you should contact them and see if they can help you."

That sounded a little better and some hope came back into my heart.

I walked to the men's barracks to look for Bruno. He was busy at his bunk putting some things together to get ready for the trip. In the past year he had been able to accumulate some additional clothing as well as toiletries and an extra pair of shoes. He gathered it all in a cardboard box. When he saw me, he put his arms around me, and crying, I told him what happened.

"How will I be able to find Mother and Renee among all these people? They shouldn't have done this to us!"

Again he brought comfort to me: "Don't despair, little Elga! I am sure you will find them, and I will help you." Then he added, "Go to your quarters now, and get your things together, too. I will see you tomorrow and we shall try to stay together."

A warm feeling went from my heart toward him. I hugged him, and kissed him on the cheek. At the same time, pleasant thoughts of Dad came to me and I wished I could stay with Bruno. Did I start feeling real love for him, or was it my loneliness that made me seek companionship?

On the way back to my barracks I wondered what would happen to us once we were in Germany. Bruno's home was somewhere in the Eastern Zone, and he had mentioned earlier that he planned to go there. Mother, Renee and I had no certain destination and would have to leave it up to fate where we would go. Would I see Bruno again after we parted in Germany?

But I could not worry about that now. My first concern was to find Mother and Renee, and I was determined not to give up!

Chapter Twenty

The Journey – Home?

The wake-up siren sounded at dawn the next morning. There was an element of joyful excitement in the air and a buzzing action engulfed the whole camp. However, the sky didn't seem to share the joyous feelings. Heavy rain clouds darkened the horizon and the light made its way very slowly into the gloomy day.

I tried to sort out my emotions. I, too, was joyous that this miserable life should finally come to an end, but my feelings were overshadowed by the fact that Mother and Renee had been separated from me. What was I going to do if I was unable to find them in Prague? For a whole year we had gone through hardship and agony together. And now, when the situation started to turn for the better, we were apart, unable to experience the happiness as a family.

In spite of the pleasant thought to be free again, I was bitter and depressed. I tried desperately to get rid of my sorrowful emotions by thinking happy thoughts. After all, we did get out of this alive! In spite of Renee's illnesses, she had recovered well both times, and Mother had regained some of her strength in the last couple of months.

I had been spared from the Russian rapes and, in spite of several severe beatings, I was fairly well off just being alive. But all these good sides of the happenings during the past year could not wipe out this last outrageous action – separating our little family at the last moment.

My thoughts went to Bruno as I tied the Russian long johns, my comb, toothbrush, soap, my skirt and a few other essentials I had acquired, into the blanket. He was the only one left to talk to, and I hoped that at least for the trip to Prague I could be with him.

I walked to the mess hall to join the other inmates for our last breakfast. Gerlinde was standing in the line before me with her little boy.

"Are we really going to be free?" she asked with tears in her eyes, clutching little Juergen. "I have a hard time believing it. I have to find Gerhard's and my parents as soon as we are in Germany. I knew he had an uncle in Munich and I will try to contact him right away. I just wish my little Kurt was with me – I miss him so!"

She was babbling like a little brook, and her words were partly drowned between laughter and tears.

"I don't know what I am going to do," I said when I finally got a word in. "I have to see first that I find my mother and sister. Then we might contact my mother's brother in Wuerthemberg. But I will have to wait and see how things develop and where they will send us."

Then the evacuation began.

It was almost exactly one year to the day after World War II had ended, the third of May 1946. Line-up again, a short walk to the train depot, and loading into freight cars.

There were not as many leaving as there had been when we arrived here nine months ago. Half of the prisoners had been shipped out two days before, and many were left in the big hole at the far end of the camp. Some were sick, some even too sick to walk. Those prisoners were on stretchers. But spirits were high and even though nobody knew where destiny was going to take us, I was hoping this would be the end of our imprisonment.

Bruno had joined me, and together we walked up the plank into the boxcar. Looking around, I saw several men and women walking as couples, and all of a sudden I had to laugh.

"You know, Bruno," I chuckled, "this looks like the loading of Noah's Ark. A pair of each!"

"I sure am glad you still have your sense of humor," Bruno marveled. "You know, you are a remarkable young woman!"

I was a little embarrassed, but flattered at his words. It felt good to have someone talk pleasantly to me.

This trip was different from the one nine months ago. We were not squeezed in as tightly as then, and there was room enough to sit on the floor. A number of people even had some luggage to carry, and their acquired pieces of clothing and blankets were packed in bundles and boxes. There were no guards posted at the end of each car.

It was an exciting day, and shouting, laughing and crying filled the air. It was hard to wait for the train to depart. Finally, shaking and rattling, it started to move. First, very slowly, then picking up speed, heading in a northerly direction.

All day we rode, stopping frequently for no apparent reason in the middle of nowhere. The train took us through Beneshov without stopping. Other towns went by.

Looking out through the openings in the walls, I began to see familiar landmarks as we approached Prague. By the time we reached the city, it was dark and the only things visible were streetlights in straight rows going from one end to the other, and across.

A strange feeling came over me. This had been my home for eleven years. Good times and not so good times were in my memory, and I came to realize I had lost it all forever.

And somewhere here Dad was buried in a big hole with many others! I burst into tears and again I thought my heart would break.

"Dear Lord," I prayed, while Bruno stroked my hair. "Please let me find Mother and Renee! I couldn't bear losing them, too!"

The train slowed down and came to a halt. We had stopped at a suburban station. The doors rolled open and unloading began.

Again we had to walk through the streets of Prague with hostile crowds lining the sidewalks. And again, much like on the first day of our arrest, we were guided into the empty classrooms of a large school.

I was eager to start my search for Mother and Renee right away, but since it was late in the evening, we were forced to stay in our assigned rooms. Men were separated from the women again, and Bruno was taken to a different room.

"I shall see you tomorrow morning!" he called out as he left.

There was a line in the hallway where ladies with Red Cross ribbons on their arms served us some thick soup and a tasty sandwich before we settled down for the night.

The next morning, after a restless sleep on the hard floor, I was awake as soon as the daylight broke through the dirty window. After a hasty breakfast of a slice of bread and some coffee, we lined up again to be registered.

The commandant in Bistrice was right; they did keep records: name, birth date, where we were form originally, and which camp we had been in for the past year.

It was in a long line, and when I finally

stepped up to the table to give my data I was so excited I could hardly speak. They had to have some information about Mother and Renee! I gave my name, intending to explain my situation.

"Look, girl," the man at the desk said. "Can't you see how busy we are? We have to register every one of you people. Do you really think I can, or want to waste my time to search for your family?" And with an impatient motion of his hand, he urged me to step aside to make room for the next person.

I suppose I have to try it on my own! I decided, and started my quest.

Walking from room to room to ask fellow prisoners, and calling out Mother's and Renee's names, I ran into Bruno.

"Let me help you look," he offered, when I told him that I could not get any help from the volunteer.

We split up, each taking a floor in our search.

Strangely enough, nobody stopped me as I investigated dozens of rooms. There were countless people in long lines to be registered, all unfamiliar faces. A small number of guards were standing around, but they seemed to have little function inside the building.

As the day went on, the hustle and bustle died down a bit, and the lines by the registration tables became shorter. My search had been completely unsuccessful and I was desperately discouraged.

Bruno came back, and he too had no success to report.

I was close to tears again. Before I headed back to my designated room I encouraged myself: 'I will give it one more try!' and stepping up to one of the tables, I requested tearfully: "Please, can you find somebody for me? I lost my mother."

There was a woman at the table, another Red Cross lady. She looked at me. Her face was exhausted, apparently she had worked all day at this reception, and I was not sure what kind of response I was going to get from her. But before she could do or say anything, the person next to her jumped up.

"Elgi!" she yelled. And just like in the dark cell in Prague on the first day of our arrest, we fell into each other's embrace. We laughed and cried, and the miracle that seemed so far away just a short while ago had come true.

I could hardly believe it; it was really Renee!

"Nothing can separate us now," she stated, and with jubilant hearts, we ran up to the third floor where Mother was standing at a window looking out into the clear day.

"Look, Mutti! Look who I found," Renee cried out. And for a moment I thought Mother was going to faint. She was so pale and thin, I knew at once she was not well. She sank to her knees and Renee and I joined her on the floor, hugging in one tightly knit triangle.

Nobody spoke and the other women in the room shared our joy with tears.

In spite of all the wishing and praying, it was hard to comprehend that the miracle actually had come true. For a miracle it was, and nobody could have predicted that outcome. We spent one more night in that school, and I had no objection from any of the guards to move to the third floor to join my family.

The next morning, at dawn again, a long trek of men, women and children moved again through the streets of Prague toward a railroad station, this time a freight depot on the outskirts of the city. Loading began again. We were joined by Bruno and we held onto each other's hands so tightly that it hurt. But for nothing in the world were we going to lose each other again.

When we were finally situated in the boxcars – hopefully for the last time – a whistle blew, and the train set in motion.

It was morning now, and the sun rose brightly in the sky. I thought about the future. What was it going to bring for us? The uncertainty bothered me; everything was so unpredictable!

But as I looked at Mother and Renee, a warm feeling embraced me. We were together again, and I knew we would face and conquer whatever was in store for us, as we had done for the last twelve months.

With God's help and our determination, we would start a new life. Maybe in a new world!

As we left the "Golden City," and the houses disappeared in the distance, melancholy settled in my heart.

Goodbye, dear Daddy, and all I had come to love and still love so dearly!

CHAPTER TWENTY-ONE

THEN WHAT HAPPENED?

After her release from the Czechoslovakian detention camp, Elga Marianne Fuchs lived with her mother and sister Renee in Germany for eight years, but they never felt at home there. Bruno joined Elga a year after their release. The two married and had a daughter, born in 1948. The marriage, however, did not last and shortly after the baby was born, Bruno took off. He returned only when Elga filed for divorce and he unsuccessfully tried to fight it.

Elga's sister, Renee, was able to secure a job with the American occupation office in Germany and with that connection eventually receive a work contract through a visiting American.

ELGA HUKE

Renee immigrated to the United States in 1952. She soon found sponsors for the rest of her family and applied for visas for her mother, for Elga, and Elga's daughter. In November 1954, the three joined Renee in Minnesota, USA. Elga remarried and had two more children.

Elga Marianne Fuchs Huke now makes her home in Oregon, where her daughter and her younger son also reside. The older son lives in Colorado where he is raising Elga's two grandsons.

Elga Marianne Fuchs Huke, 2005

photo © John Curtis Crawford